HIGHER
Administration
course notes

Caroline Patterson ✕ Moira Stephen

Text © 2007 Caroline Patterson and Moira Stephen
Design and layout © 2007 Leckie & Leckie
Cover photo © Image Bank/Getty
Cover design by Caleb Rutherford

03/230911

ISBN 978-1-84372-286-1

Published by
Leckie & Leckie Ltd
An imprint of HarperCollins*Publishers*
Westerhill Road, Bishopbriggs, Glasgow G64 2QT
T: 0844 576 8126   F: 0844 576 8131
leckieandleckie@harpercollins.co.uk   www.leckieandleckie.co.uk

Special thanks to
Project One Publishing Solutions, Edinburgh (Project management and editing)
The Partnership Publishing Solutions (Design and page layout)
Ellustration (Illustrations)

A CIP Catalogue record for this book is available from the British Library.

Acknowledgements
Leckie & Leckie has made every effort to trace all copyright holders.
If any have been inadvertently overlooked, we will be pleased to make the necessary arrangements.

We would like to thank the following for permission to reproduce their material:
Getty Images for the image on page 25; Investors in People (www.investorsinpeople.co.uk) for the use of their logo on page 66, reproduced with kind permission of Investors in People.

CONTENTS

UNIT 1 ADMINISTRATIVE SERVICES

INTRODUCTION

Welcome to Leckie & Leckie's **Higher Administration *Course Notes***. This book will prove invaluable as you study the course. It will assist you with clear and concise points and explanations to complement your class work and help you with your homework. It will also be extremely useful when revising for your internal assessments, prelims and the final exam.

This book will provide you with coverage of all eight topics within the Higher Administration course:

Unit 1 Administrative Services

- Chapter 1 Effectiveness in the workplace
- Chapter 2 Work practices and the modern working environment
- Chapter 3 Recruiting, developing and supporting staff
- Chapter 4 Meetings
- Chapter 5 Effective customer service

Unit 2 Information Technology for Management

- Chapter 6 The role of information in decision making
- Chapter 7 The impact of ICT on work practices and management of information
- Chapter 8 Using ICT to solve business problems

Internal assessment

Throughout your course you will be asked to sit internal assessments in each of the two units.

Administrative Services
The internal assessment for Administrative Services is a series of short response questions covering topics 1–5 above, under closed book (exam) conditions within a time limit of 1 hour.

Information Technology for Management (ITFM)
There are two parts to the assessment of ITFM:

- Part 1 is a series of short response questions covering topics 6 and 7 above, under controlled, closed book conditions, within a time limit of 30 minutes.
- Part 2 is a practical assignment covering topic 8. The internal assessment will include activities using email, e-diary, presentation software and the internet as well as spreadsheet, word processing and database. The assessment must be completed within 2 hours and 30 minutes.

Notes

Email, e-diary, presentation software and the internet are not included in Chapter 8. Emphasis is purely on *final exam* preparation, that is, problem solving using spreadsheet, word processing and database applications.

Although chapter 8 does not provide course notes on email, the internet, e-diary, or presentation software, you can visit websites to help you revise these areas. Go to **www.leckieandleckie.co.uk** and then click the Learning Lab button and navigate to the Higher Administration Course Notes page to find the links to websites for these applications.

Email

Go to the website of Learn the Net, follow the link to Harness Email and work through each section. By the end you should know the benefits of using email and how to construct a message with attachments.

Internet

Next try the link to Surf the Web and work through the information presented in this section. Try the Whiz Quiz to see how much you have understood.

E-diaries

Information on e-diaries can be found at Google Calendar. Use this site to revise the types of features that you would expect to find in e-diary software.

Presentation software

Go to the website of Teach ICT. From the Video tab, select Presentations to refresh your memory on how to use presentation software.

External assessment

This consists of two papers:

- Paper 1 is a theory paper worth a total of 60 marks. It lasts for 1 hour and 20 minutes and consists of two sections.
  - Section A is based on a short case study with questions. There is no choice in this section, and you must complete **all** questions. Section A is worth 20 marks.
  - Section B consists of **five** extended response questions from which you must choose **two**. Each question is worth 20 marks. *You do not need to do all five questions – select* **two** *from those given.*
- Paper 2 is also worth 60 marks and lasts for 1 hour 20 minutes. It consists of a business problem which must be solved using spreadsheet, database and word processing software, with one task requiring integration.

General hints

Paper 1

- Read the whole paper, including instructions, before deciding which questions you wish to tackle.
- Read all the questions carefully.
- Check the question several times whilst writing your answer to ensure you keep to the point.
- Watch your time – do not spend too long on one question.
- Make sure you write in complete sentences.
- Pay attention to the command word to ensure you answer correctly. A list of the SQA command words for Administration and their meanings is shown on pages 7–10.
- Where possible, give an example to demonstrate that you know what you are talking about.
- Half marks are *never* awarded – so always make a valid point and don't waffle!

Paper 2

- Do *all* of the questions, and follow the instructions carefully as this is where you can gain marks.
- Do the questions in the order that they are presented (later questions may link back to earlier ones).
- Underline or highlight keywords and instructions in the questions so that you don't miss anything.
- Check the number of printouts that you need to provide.
- Ensure that your name is on each printout (usually in the footer) and, if instructed, any additional reference.

Command words and examples

See the examples below to get an idea of the types of questions that may be asked on *communication* and suggestions of how to answer the questions, bearing in mind the *command word* in each question.

Command word	Definition/meaning
State	Listing or bullet points would be acceptable here.

Sample question

State two methods of electronic communication that an organisation may use.

Sample answer

● Email

● Mobile phones

Command word	Definition/meaning
Suggest	More than just naming or stating. Put forward a recommendation or advise on a course of action.

Sample question

Suggest two methods of electronic communication that an organisation may use.

Sample answer

Email – now one of the most popular methods of electronic communication for business and personal use. Especially useful when working across time zones, or when you don't actually need to speak to someone immediately.

Web pages/Internet – useful for information you want to communicate to customers, e.g. product information.

Command word	Definition/meaning
Outline	Identify the main features and give a brief description where appropriate.

Sample question

Outline two methods of electronic communication that an organisation may use.

Sample answer

Email – is a fast and effect method of communication as it can be sent at any time of the day or night, it can be accessed from anywhere in the world with an internet connection, and files and documents can be attached to email messages.

Mobile phones – allow employees to keep in contact with the organisation when they are not in the office. Text messages can be sent and received if signals are weak or non-existent. Voice messages can be left and some phones will allow access to the internet.

Command word	Definition/meaning
Describe	Give a description and an example

Sample question

Describe how email can help improve communication between an organisation and its customers.

Sample answer

Email provides a very quick and inexpensive way of communicating with customers. It could be used to inform a customer of how an order is progressing, or to give details of delivery plans. It could also be used to receive orders from customers. It makes communication with customers relatively easy and if used properly could lead to improved customer relations.

Command word	Definition/meaning
Explain	Give a definition and then an example as to how something may or may not be affected.

Sample question

Explain why an organisation would advertise on the internet.

Sample answer

By advertising on the internet an organisation will reach a global audience 24 hours a day, 7 days a week, every day of the year. They can cut out the middle man and reduce storage costs. They can easily update details and prices of their products, and so keep ahead of the competition. They could easily diversify into other closely related products.

Command word	Definition/meaning
Discuss	Give advantages and disadvantages where possible. Use examples to expand your answer, and if necessary give a conclusion to your answer.

Sample question

Discuss ways in which the internet could be used to communicate with clients.

Sample answer

The internet could be used to publish information on company products so that potential customers could browse the company's product range at a time that suited them. This would give the company a shop window 24 hours a day, 7 days a week, and also give the company access to customers across the globe – without the expense of opening new premises, employing extra staff and incurring other costs associated with having a physical shop front.

As well as showcasing products, an e-commerce site could be established so that orders could be taken from customers, thus making it easy for them to place an order at a time that suited them.

A company could use the internet to host a page of 'Frequently Asked Questions' to communicate the answers to regularly asked questions to potential customers.

A company would have to employ a specialist or train someone to set up and manage the website, and once set up it would be important to keep the site up to date. There is the disadvantage that technical problems could result in the site being 'down', during which time no-one would be able to access the site and place orders or find out the answer to a question – but overall most companies would find it advantageous to use the internet to communicate with clients.

Command word	Definition/meaning
Compare	You must be able to compare the similarities or differences between the items, again giving a conclusion if necessary. A key word that you can use in this type of question is *whereas*.

Sample question

Compare the limitations of email with mobile phones as forms of electronic communication.

Sample answer

With email, limitations include:

- technical problems may mean not being able to access email when necessary
- the person receiving the email might not always check their mail box regularly
- sometimes attachments are forgotten or left off the message
- it is not a secure means of communication
- sometimes the amount of 'junk' received can be very time consuming.

Whereas with mobile phones the limitations are:

- it is not always possible to get clear reception all over the country
- some networks are a lot more expensive than others
- batteries need to be kept charged
- the phone can be easily misplaced, stolen or lost
- the phone can be annoying and disturbing to others if being used in a public place or on public transport.

Command word	Definition/meaning
Justify	You must be able to give reasons why a certain course of action is being taken.

Sample question

Justify the use of email and e-diaries to communicate with colleagues when planning meetings.

Sample answer

Email could be used to send out the notice of meeting, agenda and also minutes of the previous meeting and any other papers required for the meeting.

The use of email for this would be justified as:

- the same email could be sent to many people at the same time, thus saving time
- no papers would need to be printed out, thus saving printing and material costs
- recipients could collect and read the meeting documents at a time and place that suited them
- there is a record of who has been contacted.

The use of **e-diaries** could be justified as:

- the organiser could check the e-diaries online to help them find a suitable time for a meeting. This would allow them to select a date and time that would suit most people
- an electronic invitation to a meeting could automatically update the recipient's e-diary on acceptance – so the recipient wouldn't forget to put it in their diary and miss the meeting
- e-diaries often have a reminder facility – so this could be set to remind attendees that the meeting was starting soon, so they wouldn't forget
- recipients would be warned if the meeting time clashed with any other appointment in their diary, so they would know that they had to take some action to sort the problem out.

Command word	Definition/meaning
Implications	You should be able to state what the likely outcome of a particular action will be in the longer term, either on a person or on an organisation.

Sample question

What are the possible **implications** of an organisation **not** adopting electronic methods of communication?

Sample answer

There are many implications (mostly negative) for an organisation that does not use electronic communication methods, including:

- Information will take longer to reach them than it otherwise would. This may mean that they do not have the information in time to make important decisions, so wrong decisions may be made and the profitability of the organisation suffers.
- Potential customers find it too difficult and time consuming to get in touch with them, so they lose out on business as the customers prefer to order from someone else online.
- The company cannot contact its customers quickly, so they don't find out that a delivery has been cancelled or will be late – and this will frustrate the customer who may then decide to take their business elsewhere. A text or an email to update a customer can lead to improved customer relations.
- Potential employees will often job hunt and apply for jobs via the internet – any company that does not use this method of advertising vacancies and recruiting may be missing out on reaching quality employees.
- Letters and papers take longer to distribute via traditional mail – and traditional mail may take days to reach other countries. Companies may give the impression of being inefficient if they cannot communicate information quickly with other companies, e.g. customers or suppliers.
- Companies may not be able to access the information they are looking for if they don't search it out online.

So, not embracing electronic methods of communication could have many serious implications for an organisation.

Command word	Definition/meaning
Consequences	You must be able to identify the initial impact of the action being followed.

Sample question

What would be the **consequences** for an organisation if they had not backed up their email system and it was attacked by a virus?

Sample answer

- By not taking a back-up of their email system data would be lost, e.g. minutes or records of meetings.
- This would mean that deadlines may be missed because there would be no online diary to give prompts to staff.
- Staff training would be needed to ensure that staff know how to avoid transferring viruses.
- There may be an increase in staffing costs as more technical support of the IT system may be needed and more staff may need to be employed to reinstate the missing data.
- Customer orders or enquiries may be lost leading to a reduction in profit.
- The company's reputation may suffer as being unreliable.
- Staff may become disillusioned having to redo work.

Note: *Discuss*, *Compare*, *Justify*, *Consequences* and *Implications* are the most difficult command words to address. Most marks will be awarded to questions using these words. Make sure you understand how to respond – and do not simply list the key points.

How to use this book

Quick Questions

In each section throughout the book there are quick questions to test your knowledge and understanding of what you have just read. These questions will also help to prepare you for the internal assessment. Solutions to these questions are on pages 114–120.

Extended Response Questions

At the end of each chapter you will find extended response questions. These are not past paper questions, but are similar, and should allow you to practise the type of responses you should make in the exam. Look carefully at the mark allocation and remember that key command words are shown in bold italics in each question. Solutions to these questions are on pages 121–124.

Hint

Make a note of all these exam and study hints as they will help you with your revision.

Internet Research

Throughout the book you will be directed to variety of useful websites. These sites provide additional material to help you consolidate and enhance your knowledge of the topic that you have been studying. Take some time to explore these sites.

Links to these sites and other websites relating to Higher Administration can be found at: **www.leckieandleckie.co.uk** by clicking on the Learning Lab button and navigating to the Higher Administration Course Notes page.

UNIT 1 ADMINISTRATIVE SERVICES

1 EFFECTIVENESS IN THE WORKPLACE

The role of the administrator

Administration is probably the most important function in any organisation. But what does administration involve?

- **Communicating:** answering the telephone, responding to email, dealing with faxes, texting, audio conferencing.
- **Keeping records:** maintaining diaries, reports, logbooks.
- **Providing and storing information:** filing and retrieving correspondence from both manual and electronic systems.
- **Presenting information:** word processing, using spreadsheets and databases and other specialised software as required by the organisation, for example, accounting, project management, desk top publishing, etc.
- **Interpersonal skills:** reception duties, dealing with internal and external customers to the organisation.
- **Using systems and procedures:** mail both internal and external, reprographics, photocopying, printing, binding, laminating.

Skills and qualities of a senior administrator

The duties of a senior administrator include **planning**, **organising** and **supervising** the roles involved in administration. This means that you would need to be able to:

- **delegate:** give others the responsibility and authority to carry out tasks
- **make decisions:** be accountable to senior management for operational decisions
- **develop systems and procedures:** to ensure the smooth and efficient running of the administration department
- **motivate:** encourage and organise the work of others
- **control:** ensure that there is a monitoring and evaluation procedure in place so that weaknesses can be identified. Changes can then be made to improve the allocation of resources or change procedures to meet required needs.

- Quick to learn?
- Attention to detail?
- Good organisational skills?
- Self-motivated but also a team player?
- Good customer skills?
- Flexible and adaptable to change?
- Good knowledge of business software?
- Ability to solve problems?
- Tact and initiative?
- Good communication skills and enthusiastic?

Hint

You should be able to *compare* the duties of a junior and a senior administrative assistant, making sure that you describe differences in what each one will do.

Recruiting staff

Finding an employee who has all the necessary skills and qualities is a difficult task. Organisations need to make sure that jobs are advertised in the right place to attract the best candidates. Jobs can be advertised:

- **internally** within the organisation, using intranet, bulletin boards, newsletters
- **externally** in newspapers, specialised journals, job centres, internet, schools and colleges.

Many organisations are constantly changing and when an employee leaves they do not always replace 'like with like'. Often a **job evaluation/analysis** will take place which will look at what duties are involved in the job role. These will be analysed and it may be that instead of advertising the position, the duties are reassigned to existing staff or a new job is created that is more in line with what the organisation may need at that time.

In order to identify what is required in a job, a **job description** will be produced. In addition, there will be a **person specification**. Both of these documents are very important in the recruitment stages as they clearly identify what the organisation is seeking in prospective candidates.

Job advertisement

The job advertisement gives the most basic information. It will not always mention the salary, but it will usually include the essential qualities and skills required for the post.

ADMINISTRATIVE ASSISTANT

Location: Aberdeen, busy city centre office.

Salary: £18,383 (35 hours per week).

Requires a well organised and motivated team player.

Administrative responsibilities include dealing with enquiries, word processing, diary management, arranging meetings, minute taking, financial duties, record management and general administration. Previous experience in a similar role desirable.

For an application form and job description, telephone 01224 367 5676.

Closing date for post is **19 October 2008**.

Job description

The purpose of a job description is to allow the employee to know what is involved in the job. It also allows the employer to account for the tasks that are expected to be performed. It is given to prospective applicants to help them write their application and prepare for the interview.

The job description on page 14 is very simple. Some will be more complicated, but as you can see it contains details of the job title, their line manager, where they may be located, the purpose of the job and duties and responsibilities.

Job descriptions should be living documents that are updated annually to reflect any changes in the job and what the post-holder is expected to do.

There will usually be a statement at the bottom of the job description asking the post-holder to carry out any other duties as required by their line manager and relevant to the post

Job description

Job title	Senior Administrator
Responsible to	General Manager
Location	Aberdeen Office
Job purpose	To organise resources and provide business information and support to internal and external customers

Duties	Responsibilities
Data management	Prepare and provide management information and reports
Customer guidance	Provide customer services to required standard
Resource management	Efficient and timely use of appropriate resources
Delivery of services	Plan and organise own work and co-ordinate with other team members Ensure allocated work completed on time to required standard
Administrative services	Work as member of a team Complete tasks to required standards by set deadlines Schedule meetings and events Make travel arrangements Diary management Support senior colleagues
Financial transactions	Monitor and reconcile financial transactions as detailed by General Manager
Hours of work	35 hours per week
Rate of pay	£18,383 (subject to review)

Person specification

Finding the right person for the job can be difficult, so it is important to design a job or person specification which will detail the skills and qualities that the ideal candidate must have. It should also show which ones would be helpful but not essential.

The interviewer will use this document during the interview as it makes it easier to compare one candidate with another.

Person specification

Quality	Essential	Desirable
Personal effectiveness	Good communication and customer skills Decision making Positive attitude Self-motivated Flexible	Sense of humour
Qualifications and experience	HNC/D in relevant area or SVQ Level 3 Financial record keeping	Experience in a similar position Clean driving licence
Skills	Sound knowledge of Word, Excel and Outlook	Knowledge of Access and shorthand for minute taking

Hint

Can you state the purpose of a *job description* and a *person specification*, and give details of what is contained in each?

1 Outline two key differences between the roles of a senior and junior administrator.
2 Identify six duties routinely carried out by office staff.
3 List four important personal qualities of a senior administrator.
4 Describe the difference between an essential quality and a desirable one as would appear on a person specification.
5 Explain the term 'job evaluation'.

Aims, objectives and targets

It is important within any organisation that staff share the management's vision. It is the duty of the senior administrative assistant to set both personal and departmental targets to enable the organisation to meet its long-term goals. Departmental targets will only be achieved by employees working as a team and to their own personal targets.

These targets will be based on a number of factors and will be recorded in a variety of different documents, as shown in the table below.

Type of document	Description
Gantt chart	Used by managers to show comparisons between work planned and work accomplished in relation to time schedules. Looks a bit like a bar graph. Key target dates will be marked on the chart – these are sometimes called milestones.
'To do' list	Usually a note to yourself – sometimes on sticky bits of paper – showing a list of tasks that need to be done.
Priorities list	The same list of tasks but this time put in an order showing which task needs to be tackled first.
Action plan	A document which identifies what should be done by whom, with expected completion dates.
Electronic diary (e-diary)	Useful for arranging meetings as days, weeks and months can be seen at one glance, and the e-diaries of all participants can be seen at the same time. Most e-diaries have electronic task lists.
Personal development plan (PDP)	A formal document which records aims and objectives that need to be met by training or development. This helps the employee to meet the targets set. Some organisations also encourage employees to record personal aims; although not a requirement of the job, these may enhance the employee's confidence and well-being. The PDP is often discussed annually, then reviewed perhaps once or twice a year to help monitor performance.

Targets need to be SMART

S	**Specific:** They must state exactly what has to be done.
M	**Measurable:** They must state how much/what size, so you know you can reach them.
A	**Agreed:** They must be agreed with the line manager, usually in a discussion as part of the PDP.
R	**Realistic:** They should be achievable but still be a challenge.
T	**Timed:** It is important that key dates identify when the work will be completed.

Internet Research

Visit the website of the University of Central Lancashire to access an action plan and targets and goals to try for yourself.

Links to this site and other websites relating to Higher Administration can be found at: **www.leckieandleckie.co.uk** by clicking on the Learning Lab button and navigating to the Higher Administration Course Notes page.

Dealing with changing priorities

There is no point in setting targets if no one bothers to keep to the schedule to try and achieve them. Therefore certain controls must be put in place. Monitoring targets can be done in a variety of different ways. Managers may support their employees by checking at regular intervals that the work is progressing, or by putting a more experienced member of staff in charge to act as a mentor. Occasionally audits, which are really checks on systems and procedures, may take place as a project is ongoing or even when it is complete. A report will be submitted to the manager with recommendations and action to be taken.

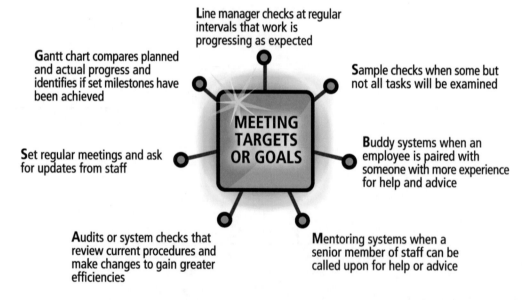

There are occasions, however, when problems occur, even though monitoring has been in place. When there are deviations, or targets are not met, then some questions need to be asked before a solution can be put in place.

Question	Solution
■ Were the targets SMART?	■ Maybe the time should have been extended.
■ Were you dependent on the actions of others?	■ Where possible this situation should be avoided.
■ Did additional tasks occur after the job started?	■ If so, find out why this happened. In future, reconsider deadlines in similar situations. Offer overtime if necessary.
■ Was the job too difficult? Did you have the right experience?	■ It is important to discuss any limitations you may feel you have at the start.
■ Were you supported?	■ Investigate sources of additional help.

Time and task management

Time management is a very important life skill. Many people find themselves frustrated with their day and this often leads to stress as they try to catch up on work that they have not managed to complete.

> Time management is not about *how much* time you spend, but *how* it is spent.

Time management is actually self-management. The skills needed to do this are the same as those mentioned for managing others on page 11 – planning, organising, delegating, directing and controlling. Time management will only work once we understand the reasons for reduced effectiveness in the workplace. These are known as **time stealers** and could be:

- interruption, whether telephone or visitors – learn to control the time spent
- meetings that take longer than necessary – set time limits
- taking on too much – delegate more tasks
- acting with incomplete information
- crisis management – reacting hastily to emergency situations rather than having plans in place
- unclear or poor communication
- inability to say 'no' – don't let others offload their work on to you
- desk stress – a cluttered and untidy desk where you cannot find things
- procrastination – finding another task to do instead of starting/ completing the current one.

Effects of poor time management

- Staff become stressed and absence levels may increase
- Poor productivity – work is not produced as efficiently or to the right quality
- Morale will drop in the workforce – low job satisfaction
- An increase in accidents or unnecessary incidents
- Increased costs to management

Organisational or planning aids to help employees manage time effectively include:

- at the end of each day, prepare a priorities list and tidy your desk
- allocate tasks as must be done/needs some action/delegate
- record any appointments in a desk or electronic diary
- access email only at certain times of the day
- file regularly
- delegate tasks to others.

Delegation is very important as it helps to develop staff, improves motivation, saves time and leaves the manager free to get on with more important tasks. Unfortunately, some managers find delegation very difficult because:

- they think they can always do the job better themselves
- they have too high standards
- they are afraid of losing control.

Benefits of good time management

- Better morale and job satisfaction for employees
- Increased productivity and better quality of work produced
- Lower stress levels and less staff absence, resulting in a more communicative workforce and improved productivity
- Better relations with both internal and external clients

Internet Research

Visit the BusinessBalls or MindTools websites to find more information on time management techniques.

Links to these sites and other websites relating to Higher Administration can be found at: **www.leckieandleckie.co.uk** by clicking on the Learning Lab button and navigating to the Higher Administration Course Notes page.

LECKIE&LECKIE Learning Lab

Hint

Make sure you can discuss the implications of poor delegation.

Quick Questions 2

1. Describe two planning aids which the senior administrator could use to manage their time.
2. Explain the purpose of a personal development plan.
3. What is a time stealer? List three examples.
4. Suggest two ways an administrator could monitor targets.
5. Explain what is meant by a 'measurable target'.

Team working

Features of effective teams

Flatter organisational structures have led to an increase in **team working**. A **team** is a group of people who come together to achieve a common goal. An effective team will have good leadership and members who are all keen to take on different roles, for example:

- being responsible for set tasks
- helping the team leader to make decisions
- giving feedback at meetings and listening to others' ideas
- helping and supporting others with their tasks
- suggesting ideas and being prepared to compromise.

R. Meredith Belbin, a management theorist, suggested that there are clearly identifiable roles for team members. He suggested that, whether the team is large or small, there is someone prepared to play one or more parts, defining a team role as 'A tendency to behave, contribute and interrelate with others in a particular way.'

Effective teams need to have a balance between the people who have the ideas and those who put them into action. If the team leader is able to identify the types of individuals when starting up the team and is able to ensure a good balance, then it may be easier to manage the relationships, behaviours and characteristics of the team. Belbin's roles are:

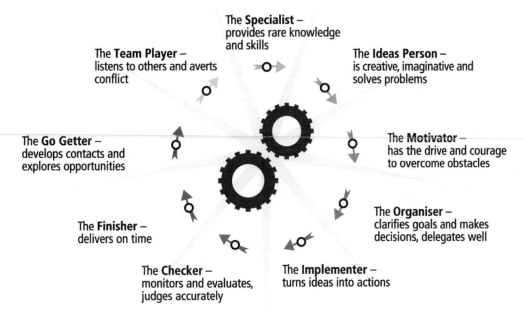

The Specialist – provides rare knowledge and skills

The Team Player – listens to others and averts conflict

The Ideas Person – is creative, imaginative and solves problems

The Go Getter – develops contacts and explores opportunities

The Motivator – has the drive and courage to overcome obstacles

The Finisher – delivers on time

The Organiser – clarifies goals and makes decisions, delegates well

The Checker – monitors and evaluates, judges accurately

The Implementer – turns ideas into actions

Stages in team development

It is thought that before teams are fully effective they go through various stages.

- **Forming:** the team members are introduced.
- **Storming:** members compete for roles; there could be some dispute and power struggles.
- **Norming:** members start working together and for each other, conflicts are resolved.
- **Performing:** the team is settled and working together.

What makes a team effective?

- Shared goals and supporting each other
- Shared knowledge
- Shared experience and skills
- Productive environment
- Ability to resolve conflict within the team

Team conflict

There are many reasons for conflict but it usually occurs when there are:

- conflicting goals: two members of the team want to go in different directions
- personal disputes: there are always people who will not get on, causing difficulties for the team
- lack of resources: not being able to put all ideas into action because there is not enough money, staff, equipment, etc.
- changing expectations: perhaps moving deadlines or the targets being changed after the work has started
- loyalty issues: affected by the relationships that exist between members of the team.

Types of team leaders

Good leaders generally have the ability to think clearly, analyse situations and make decisions. They know how to delegate, motivate and communicate. They have good social skills and can build relationships with all members of their team. Good leaders have technical proficiency, and the skills and expertise for core areas of the job. There are different forms of leadership, but it is generally recognised that the democratic leader is the preferred option.

Autocratic	This type of leader takes decisions without consultation and has very little regard for the thoughts and opinions of other colleagues or the workforce; usually found in traditional organisations.
Democratic	This type of leader is much more likely to be consultative and to encourage participative decision making.
Laissez-faire	This is the 'Let it be' leader who prefers the workforce to take their own decisions. This type of leadership can be useful in businesses where creative ideas are important but it relies heavily on good team work.

Some argue that leadership is an organisational function and not a personal quality. John Adair, a leading management theorist, identified three overlapping sets of needs that all leaders must address. He argued that there will never really be a perfect match between the three elements and that it is up to the manager to manage. This model encourages a flexible approach to leadership, with the idea that there is no 'right' style of leadership but that the style that best fits the situation should be adopted at any one time.

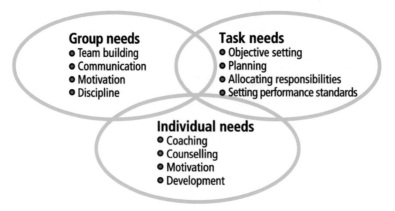

Group needs
- Team building
- Communication
- Motivation
- Discipline

Task needs
- Objective setting
- Planning
- Allocating responsibilities
- Setting performance standards

Individual needs
- Coaching
- Counselling
- Motivation
- Development

Internet Research

There are many theories about 'good leadership'. Use the internet to find out about D. McGregor and his 'X' and 'Y' Theories. Contrast these with R. Tannenbaum and W Schmidt. F. Fiedler and R. Likert also had interesting ideas. Take some notes on what these theorists thought.

What is **charisma**? Look this up on the internet. Write down the names of some leaders you think have charisma.

Benefits of effective team working

Benefits to the individual

- There is a sense of being valued and belonging
- Being able to share knowledge and increase skills by learning from others
- Increased motivation and morale
- More likely to take risks, as these are shared

Benefits to the organisation

- A multi-skilled and flexible workforce that can change and adapt to needs as required
- Employees take on more responsibility and need less supervision
- Specialisation and division of labour into different project areas
- Risks undertaken successfully can hugely benefit organisation

Hint

Make sure you can differentiate between the benefits of team work to the individual and to the organisation.

Quick Questions 3

1 List the characteristics of a successful team.
2 Which is the most successful stage of team development? Why?
3 Give two reasons why conflict may arise within a team.
4 Outline two qualities of a successful leader.
5 Using Belbin's descriptions, which role or roles would you play in a team? Give a reason for your answer.

Extended Response Questions

1 **Discuss** the methods used by a senior administrator to supervise and organise an efficient and effective workplace. [10 marks]

2 **Justify** the use of a personal development plan as a means of improving personal performance. [8 marks]

3 **Describe** three factors that might contribute to deviations from planned targets. [6 marks]

4 **Discuss** the possible **consequences** of not setting targets to the employees in an organisation. [8 marks]

5 **Identify** and **describe** three time stealers. [9 marks]

6 **Describe** the benefits and concerns individual members may have of belonging to a team. [6 marks]

Work practices

Due to changes in the working environment and in society, organisations have had to change to meet the demands of both their customers and their employees; the key word for both groups is **flexibility**.

Work practices have evolved to meet the 24/7 society we now live in. Traditional working hours of 9–5 pm have been replaced with a variety of different forms of working. It is just as common to find employees sending an email from home or the local café as it is from the office. Some organisations have also started to **outsource** their core business. This means getting another organisation to undertake work usually at a lower overall cost to the organisation and perhaps with a more skilled workforce, thus meaning the organisation needs to recruit fewer staff.

Traditional work patterns (mainly office-based)	Newer work patterns
Part-time	Homeworking, teleworking
Flexi-time	Hot-desking
Shift work	Career breaks
Job share	Non-paid leave

> **Hint**
> Make sure you can justify the use of different work practices in an organisation.

The impact of new work practices

Organisations that use a mix of these new work practices, such as hot-desking and outsourcing, have found that they can cut costs – fewer employees means they buy less equipment and they don't need as much office/work space, reducing rental costs. They have also been able to retain valued staff by introducing flexible working, which has advantages and disadvantages both to the employer and the employee, some of which are listed below.

Advantages to employer	Disadvantages to employer
■ There is a larger pool of labour so wider range of available skills	■ It can be difficult to offer training and staff development to all part-time workers
■ Ability to offer flexible work patterns may suit employees with children therefore retaining good staff	■ It is not always easy to ensure health and safety in home environment
■ Happier staff will improve morale and increase productivity	■ It is harder to organise and control a large number of part-time workers
■ Less absenteeism	■ Difficulties in communication
■ Cheaper rent/accommodation costs	■ Technical difficulties when equipment breaks down

Advantages to employee	Disadvantages to employee
■ Flexible work patterns make it easier to combine work and family life especially for single parents or carers ■ Part-time workers tend to have lower stress levels as they have some time to 'recharge' themselves on days off ■ Freedom to choose when and where to work ■ Reduction in travel ■ More accessible for people with disabilities	■ There might be fewer opportunities for staff development and training ■ There can be feelings of isolation when in the home environment ■ Hot-desking may result in depersonalisation of space, leading to a feeling of not belonging to the organisation ■ It can be more difficult to develop new relationships ■ Difficult to balance work and home commitments, need for discipline to work working hours

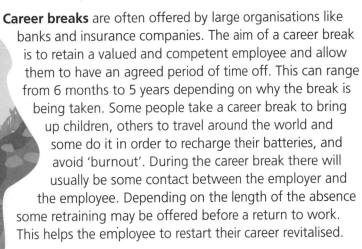

Career breaks are often offered by large organisations like banks and insurance companies. The aim of a career break is to retain a valued and competent employee and allow them to have an agreed period of time off. This can range from 6 months to 5 years depending on why the break is being taken. Some people take a career break to bring up children, others to travel around the world and some do it in order to recharge their batteries, and avoid 'burnout'. During the career break there will usually be some contact between the employer and the employee. Depending on the length of the absence some retraining may be offered before a return to work. This helps the employee to restart their career revitalised.

Another example of flexible working arrangements is granting non-paid leave to parents during school holiday periods, especially during the long summer break when parents often find it difficult to find child care.

Internet Research

Visit the Flexibility website to find out more about options for flexible working.

Links to this site and other websites relating to Higher Administration can be found at: **www.leckieandleckie.co.uk** by clicking on the Learning Lab button and navigating to the Higher Administration Course Notes page.

LECKIE&LECKIE
Learning Lab

Hint

Make sure you understand the advantages and disadvantages of flexible work patterns and can discuss the *effect* they can have on the employee and the employer.

Today, employees are faced with a variety of different working contracts. It is now very unusual to find an employee serving 25 years or more in a single organisation, as full-time, permanent contracts are increasingly rare. Nowadays no job is 'for life'. Instead there are:

- part-time contracts – can be permanent or temporary
- full-time contracts – can be permanent or temporary
- temporary contracts – for an indefinite period of time
- fixed-term contracts – will have a fixed start and end date
- outsourcing – work is contracted out either to gain services more cheaply and cost-effectively (for example, in cleaning, decorating, catering) or for specialised services (for example, payroll or call centre).

Employers use the flexibility of contracts to cover periods of boom, slump and holidays in the most efficient and effective way.

Hint
Can you compare and contrast how employers will use the different types of contracts?

Internet Research

Visit the websites of these organisations:

Department of Trade and Industry/ Department for Business, Enterprise and Regulatory Reform – to find out about the rights of part time workers

ACAS (Advisory, Conciliation and Arbitration Service) – to find out about the rights of fixed-term employees

WorkSMART – for more about workers' rights.

Links to these sites and other websites relating to Higher Administration can be found at: **www.leckieandleckie.co.uk** by clicking on the Learning Lab button and navigating to the Higher Administration Course Notes page.

The contract of employment

This is a legally enforceable agreement between the employer and the employee. Under the Employment Rights Act of 1996 an organisation is required by law to give an employee a written statement of the main terms and conditions of employment within 8 weeks of starting employment. The statement must include the following terms:

- the job title
- working hours
- required duties
- wage/salary details
- holiday details
- pension details
- discipline and grievance procedures
- date of employment.

Some terms of employment may not be written down but are **implied** by law or by **custom and practice** in the workplace. For example, the employer has an implied duty to provide a safe, secure and healthy environment. If something has been done for a period of time (for example, allowing employees to finish at midday on Christmas Eve) then this might not be written in the contract but the employee could expect it because it has become a custom.

> ### Hint
> Make sure you can state the purpose of a contract of employment and the areas that it covers.

The Act also specifies the right to an itemised pay slip and rights relating to working on a Sunday, maternity/paternity leave and the termination of employment.

Quick Questions 1

1 Outline one advantage to the employee and one to the employer of the following work practices:

   a career break   **b** flexi-time.

2 State when outsourcing work may be advantageous for an employer.

3 Suggest two reasons why hot-desking has become more popular with organisations.

4 State when an employer may use a fixed-term contract instead of a temporary contract of employment to hire an employee.

5 Explain what is meant by an 'implied' term of employment. Give an example.

The work environment

The work environment has changed greatly in the last 20 years. The building of any new work premises will take environmental factors into account and will be designed to make the best and most flexible use of the available space. There will be a mix of traditional desk areas, but there will also be **touch down** areas for using laptops and other mobile technologies, and **chill out** areas for staff to socialise. Many new builds encourage greater use of public transport by not having car parking facilities. Environmental practices – such as reduction and recycling of waste – are encouraged. Often there is very little storage space, because the increase in digitisation of paperwork and electronic file storage means fewer physical files to store. It is much more common now to find people working in large **open plan offices** (as shown in the photo) rather in smaller traditional **cellular offices** (one or two people working in their own space or room bounded by permanent walls).

Office layout

The layout and condition of the office will affect work in a number of ways. Poorly designed layout will disrupt the efficiency of the workflow. Staff should not have to walk from one end of the building to the other just to retrieve work from the shared printer. Even if staff hot-desk, it still makes sense for them to be located physically in the same department. This is often achieved by the use of partitions or screens, plants and the grouping of the furniture. Staff are motivated by pleasant surroundings and being able to access resources easily, so morale and productivity can be affected by poorly designed conditions.

> Employees who work in large open plan environments sometimes complain of illnesses such as headaches, sore throats and tiredness, which they believe are associated with the building they work in. This is known as **sick building syndrome**.

Open plan office

Advantages	Disadvantages
■ Easy to supervise ■ Savings in space and equipment ■ Staff social areas away from work areas ■ Meeting rooms for private work ■ Shared resources	■ Can be noisy ■ Unable to alter heating or lighting to suit personal requirements – often only air conditioning ■ Lack of privacy

Cellular office

Advantages	Disadvantages
■ Quiet – doors can be closed ■ Status – boss has own room ■ Privacy for one-to-one discussions ■ Ability to alter heat and light to suit personal requirements	■ Wastes space ■ More difficult to supervise and share resources ■ Uneconomic ■ Difficult to promote team work

Internet Research

Use the internet to find out more about sick building syndrome. Make notes about the syndrome, and find out how organisations can arrange the work environment to prevent it.

Ergonomics

Office **ergonomics** is about fitting the workspace environment and the employee together in the best way to prevent physical and mental health problems. Increased use of technology means that more employees use workstations with PCs and VDUs, resulting in an increase in **musculoskeletal** disorders. These are illnesses which involve muscles or the skeleton and include carpal tunnel syndrome, repetitive strain injuries, back injuries, neck and shoulder pain.

Ergonomics can help prevent, alleviate or even solve some of those illnesses. The right type of furniture and equipment, lighting, ventilation, décor, pictures, plants and personal possessions in the right place can help to create a feeling of well-being in the workplace.

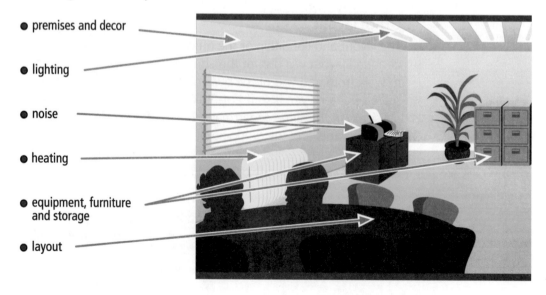

- premises and decor
- lighting
- noise
- heating
- equipment, furniture and storage
- layout

Office layout should contribute to productive and efficient workflow. The temperature, space and lighting must be comfortable for the majority of workers and comply with legal requirements. Dull or dark colours can be demotivating. Different colours can affect individuals' moods; for example blue, lemon and green are seen as restful and have a positive effect on morale and motivation. Too much noise can add to stress levels, significantly affecting the performance of some members of staff.

Internet Research

Visit the Open Ergonomics website for more information on the importance of ergonomics in the workplace. Select the Student zone tab and the Safe office practice zone. Try the risk assessment for your own workstation.

Links to this site and other websites relating to Higher Administration can be found at: **www.leckieandleckie.co.uk** by clicking on the Learning Lab button and navigating to the Higher Administration Course Notes page.

Organisational and legal requirements

Employers and the employee must follow required legislation regarding health and safety in the workplace. It is the employer's responsibility to provide information on health, safety and welfare to employees, much of which will relate to changing work practices and increased use of technology. Most organisations have their own health and safety policies and they use a number of methods to make sure that all employees are informed of their duties and responsibilities and are kept up to date.

Induction training
When they begin employment, all new employees will receive training (and supporting documentation) informing them of the company's health and safety policy.

The company intranet
Updates and copies of further documentation are posted for staff use; can be easily updated.

Notice boards/posters
Used to highlight specific policies, for example, no smoking or fire drill procedures. Must be current and relevant.

Staff development training
For first aid or dealing with fire procedures. Used when practical activities need to be observed and demonstrated.

Newsletters
For further updates or to bring issues to the attention of staff. Can be made interesting, personal and motivating, for example awarding prizes to top performing staff.

DVDs, videos, LCD screens
For training purposes or simply for information; can be set up in reception areas to reinforce knowledge.

Staff meeting
When big issues need to be discussed with specialist health and safety staff and it is important to give information quickly or to introduce new procedures.

Quizzes on a virtual learning environment (VLE)
Testing staff knowledge and understanding by means of a self-correcting quiz on the intranet or VLE saves time and staff training. Employees take the test in their own time, while the employer can check levels of understanding and provide follow-up training if necessary.

Health and safety legislation is constantly changing and being updated. You should know the main provisions of the Health and Safety at Work Act 1974 which is really like a large umbrella covering the minimum standards that need to be followed. The main regulations to be aware of are given below.

- **Health and Safety (First Aid) Regulations 1981**
  These state that there needs to be a qualified first aid person and suitable equipment to administer first aid depending on the number of employees within the organisation.

- **Workplace (Health, Safety and Welfare) Regulations 1992**
  These cover the four main areas of the workplace – the working environment, safety, facilities (for example, toilets) and maintenance of equipment and premises.

- **The Health and Safety (Display Screen Equipment) Regulations 1992**
  These regulations provide protection for employees working at workstations with VDUs and PCs. They give guidance on the length of time to work at a VDU and advice on the provision of special equipment like screen and wrist guards to avoid fatigue or strains.

- **Fire Precautions (Workplace) (Amendment) Regulations 1999**
  This legislation states that there should be means of fire detection (alarm bells) in case of fire, ways to escape, equipment to fight fires and staff trained in fire safety issues.

Note: Further legislation covering the security of information and data is described in Chapter 7 (see pages 91–94).

Breaches of health and safety legislation

Health and Safety Executive

If an organisation does not follow health and safety guidelines then the Health and Safety Executive – the body responsible for the enforcement of health and safety – can:

- enter and inspect premises – sometimes unannounced
- issue improvement notices and provide advice
- question and interview people and give warnings
- shut down premises
- fine or prosecute when necessary.

An employee who fails to comply with health and safety policies may face disciplinary procedures; depending on the seriousness of the incident, these procedures include:

- a verbal warning
- a written warning
- suspension
- fine
- dismissal
- criminal or civil prosecution.

Disciplinary procedures need to be formal and it is important that all parties know why they have been taken. When an employee is issued with a verbal warning they must be made aware of the consequences of not heeding this warning. They should know that the written warning is a second and possibly last chance before really serious action will be taken. If they are suspended from work it could ruin the employee's reputation and they may not receive any pay. A fine could also cause financial hardship but dismissal and prosecution are obviously the most serious steps in the discipline procedure and should only be taken when all other steps have been followed or if the offence is extremely serious. There should also be an appeals procedure, to give the employee the opportunity to argue their case against wrongful dismissal.

Internet Research

Visit the website of the Health and Safety Executive. This website has lots of very useful information and is an excellent way of keeping up to date with the changes in legislation. From the home page follow the links to find out what procedures need to be followed to report an incident at work. What does RIDDOR stand for? Also follow the link to find out what your rights and responsibilities as a worker are. Take notes.

Visit the Business Link website which has lots of useful information regarding working with employees. For more information on how to discipline employees, select the Employing People link.

Links to these sites and other websites relating to Higher Administration can be found at: **www.leckieandleckie.co.uk** by clicking on the Learning Lab button and navigating to the Higher Administration Course Notes page.

Quick Questions 2

1 Outline two advantages of an open plan office to the employee.
2 Explain what you understand by the term 'sick building syndrome'.
3 List four factors to consider when designing an open plan office.
4 Why has the study of ergonomics become so important in workplace design?
5 Suggest two methods employers can use to inform employees of changes to legislation.

Extended Response Questions

1 **Discuss** the possible effects on employees of moving from a traditional office to an open plan environment with hot-desking. [6 marks]

2 **Discuss** the options available to an employer to promote greater flexibility and efficiency within the workplace. [8 marks]

3 **Identify** and **describe** the checks that can be made to ensure a healthy working environment for employees and reduce the risks of illness from sick building syndrome. [8 marks]

4 **Describe** the costs and benefits of homeworking to the employer. [6 marks]

5 **Justify** the use of online training materials by employers to inform staff of updates to current legislation. [4 marks]

6 **Discuss** the possible **consequences** for an employee if they breach health and safety legislation within the organisation. [8 marks]

3 RECRUITING, DEVELOPING AND SUPPORTING STAFF

Recruitment and selection procedures

Human Resources is the functional department with responsibility for the recruitment and selection of staff. These are two different processes. **Recruitment** is about getting the right applicant to apply for a job whereas **selection** is about choosing the right person for the right job. Most organisations conduct a job evaluation/analysis before embarking on the recruitment process to fill a vacancy. (For more information on advertising jobs, job descriptions and person specifications, see pages 13–14.)

Job evaluation is a process that identifies and determines:

- the duties of a particular job
- the skills required for the job
- the importance of the skills identified for the job, for example, whether essential or desirable.

It is important to be clear that job evaluation is the analysis of the job, not the person, and its main purpose is to help to establish procedures for the selection, training and performance appraisal for that post.

The first question to be asked is: 'Do we need to replace this post?' Whether the answer is yes or no determines the next steps.

"Yes, it is essential that a lifeguard can swim..."

Yes	No
■ Prepare job description	■ Is it to be outsourced?
■ Draw up person specification	■ Can it be shared among existing staff?
■ Prepare advertisement	■ Does the role still exist at all?
■ Interview candidates	

An organisation should 'take stock' of its employees regularly and have data on these aspects of its workforce:

- **age and sex**

  This allows the organisation to take demographic changes in the population into account and to highlight any imbalances or problem areas.

- **skills**

  This will help identify areas of weakness or areas where some people may need to be retrained.

- **labour turnover**

  This will reveal problem areas and the flexibility of staff.

- **ethnic minorities and disabled**

  How many are represented within the workforce? This information can demonstrate whether the organisation is inclusive in its recruitment policies.

- **a succession plan**

  Who is available to succeed whom within the organisation's hierarchy?

If the organisation intends to recruit locally then it needs to be aware of external factors affecting the workforce, such as:

- the socio-economic group living near or within the location
- the pattern of immigration or emigration to or from the area
- plans for new residential developments
- the nature of the educational output from the local schools
- local unemployment levels
- competition from other companies in the area
- transport and infrastructure.

Hint

Remember that when a vacancy exists for a job, it is not automatically filled either by an internal or an external applicant. Organisations will take the opportunity to evaluate the duties and role of that job before they decide to fill the post.

Internal and external advertising of vacancies

There are advantages and disadvantages of advertising both internally (within the organisation) and externally (outwith the organisation). If a clerical worker or office junior is required then this post may easily be filled by recruiting through the local job centre. However, if the organisation requires a specialist, or a managing director, then advertising in the national press will be more appropriate. Sometimes an organisation will know who they want for a specific job and they will approach that person directly and ask them to apply for the job. This is known as **headhunting**.

Internal recruitment	
Advantages	**Disadvantages**
■ Less expensive ■ Employee is known to the firm so their knowledge and skills are known ■ Greater use being made of existing workforce ('homegrown talent'), increasing flexibility ■ Provides opportunities within the organisation, improving morale within the existing workforce	■ Does not allow for the introduction of new/fresh talent ■ Can promote favouritism and encourage some employees to only work with certain managers ■ May be difficult to find the right replacement for the vacancy

External recruitment	
Advantages	**Disadvantages**
■ Better chance of getting the right person for the job ■ Introduces new/fresh ideas and skills ■ Opportunity to increase diversity	■ More expensive ■ Recruitment process may take longer ■ May upset existing employees ■ New employee may need extra training

Selection procedures

A good advertisement and a well-designed application form should attract a good response but sifting through a large number of applications can be a difficult and time-consuming process. Many organisations now provide online application forms to speed up the process.

A properly conducted job evaluation may help the selection process because it will have identified or developed the following:

- minimum requirements (education and/or experience) for screening applicants
- interview questions
- selection tests/instruments (for example, written tests, oral tests, job simulations)
- applicant appraisal/evaluation forms
- orientation materials for applicants.

Some applicants will send a **curriculum vitae** (CV) along with their application form. A CV is a summary of their qualifications and experience. Organisations often remove the front sheet from application forms (the usual place for personal details such as marital status or date of birth) so as to follow **equal opportunity** guidelines when selecting suitable applicants for the next stage in the recruitment process. The selection of candidates will then be made entirely on qualifications and experience and not affected by personal details such as age, marital status, religion or sex.

Equal opportunity guidelines cover various areas which are particularly sensitive in the recruitment and selection of staff. In general, it is unlawful to treat one person less favourably than another, wholly or mainly on the grounds of their sex, marital status, race, nationality, colour, ethnic or national origin, disability, age, or religion. Important legislation includes:

- **Equal Pay Act 1970**
  This states that men and women must be given equal pay for equal work or work of equal value.
- **Sex Discrimination Act 1975 and 1985**
  This states that both men and women have the same right to the same job, and that employers must show that they treat men and women equally.
- **Race Relations Act 1976**
  This states that a person cannot be discriminated against because of the colour of their skin or their ethnic origin.
- **Disability Discrimination Act 1995**
  This protects the rights of disabled people, requiring businesses to take steps to make their premises and job opportunities available to all disabled persons. It is unlawful to 'unjustifiably' discriminate against an individual on the grounds of their disability in relation to recruitment, promotion, training, benefits, terms and conditions of employment.

The employer must always ensure that neither direct nor indirect discrimination takes place.

- **Direct discrimination** is when one person is treated less favourably than a person of the opposite sex, religion, age, etc. An advertisement that asked for a 'young motivated woman' discriminates directly against men and older people.
- **Indirect discrimination** is when a condition or requirement is applied equally to both sexes but the application of that condition may make it harder for one particular group to comply. A condition that 'all staff must wear skirts'

discriminates indirectly against men, whereas 'staff must be at least 1.75 metres tall in order to reach equipment' discriminates indirectly against most women.

Once candidates have been **shortlisted** (selected for interview), then the selection interviews need to be arranged. For reasons of practicality (time and money), most organisations will limit the number of candidates to be interviewed (often between four and eight candidates).

Interviews can take several different formats. There may be a one-to-one interview between the interviewer and candidate; a number of interviews may be involved, for example, a preliminary one and then a second more formal one; or it might involve a presentation in front of a panel, with questions and answers to follow.

Internet Research

Visit the website for Nottingham University, and follow the link to Recruitment & Selection. This site covers the process of how an educational establishment recruits and selects staff. There are exercises for you to try (like writing a job description) and a quiz on equal opportunity legislation.

Links to this site and other websites relating to Higher Administration can be found at: **www.leckieandleckie.co.uk** by clicking on the Learning Lab button and navigating to the Higher Administration Course Notes page.

Hint
Make sure you know the difference between direct and indirect discrimination.

The interview

Experienced interviewers make sure that they are well prepared. They will:

- book a room and arrange the seating
- read all the necessary documentation
- if appropriate, speak to the panel and check that everyone agrees on questions
- control the interview so that it runs to time
- put the candidate at ease.

The interview is believed to be one of the best methods of selection. It allows both the interviewer and the interviewee to meet and discuss issues face to face. It also allows the candidate to view the work premises – which may be better or worse than expected. The interview has some disadvantages, however, mainly that interviewers can form hasty impressions based on irrelevant factors (for example, the colour or style of a candidate's hair), and interviewees may be very nervous and not perform to their full potential.

Interviewers should have a checklist that enables them to grade candidates fairly. The interviewer can use this checklist to justify their decisions, and demonstrate why a particular candidate was or was not offered the post. Sometimes tests are conducted at interviews. The different types of tests can help when choosing between candidates.

Tests

- **Intelligence tests:** general knowledge, numeracy and literacy
- **Aptitude tests:** ability to perform certain duties, such as prioritising tasks
- **Attainment tests:** spelling or typing a set number of words per minute
- **Personality/psychometric tests:** explore the candidate's personality and thinking processes
- **Medical tests:** check that the candidate is fit for the type of job, for example, teacher or police officer

An effective interview is one where the interviewer:

- quickly establishes a rapport with the candidate
- listens to what is said
- asks 'open' questions for example 'Can you give me an example of when you showed leadership qualities?'
- summarises and evaluates the candidate's responses.

Once a decision has been made about offering a candidate the job, it is important that references and other employment checks are carried out, such as Disclosure Scotland (a check made on the personal background of people who will be working with children). Referees should be contacted to authenticate what they said in their reference. All unsuccessful candidates should be informed in writing.

Quick Questions 1

1 Outline the purpose of job evaluation.
2 Suggest when a psychometric test may be used at interview.
3 Explain why the page containing personal details may be removed from an application form before selection takes place.
4 Describe three different types of interview a candidate could face.
5 Suggest a reason for carrying out employment checks after the interview.

Staff development

Appraisal

Many organisations use an appraisal scheme to identify staff development and training requirements.

By conducting appraisals of employee performance, organisations improve their chances of attaining their key operational goals. Employees who know what and how much is expected of them are likely to be more effective than those who are unclear about their role. The appraisal must be:

- objective – it is not a forum for raising problems and moans
- participative – both employer (usually the line manager) and employee take part
- considered – it should take account of the strategic aims of the organisation
- developmental – it should help to develop the employee both personally and professionally.

Although the appraisal can be linked to target setting, most employees are not keen when it is related to **performance-related pay** (PRP).

Successful appraisals aim to:

- identify and match business and personal objectives
- discover the work potential of employees, especially with regards to promotion
- identify training needs
- control and monitor performance
- assist individuals with their own self-development
- improve employee motivation by understanding and recognising their needs
- review salaries or payment methods
- check effectiveness of current practices, for example, recruitment and training
- update the job description.

What does an appraisal involve?

It is a meeting between the employee and the line manager where a performance evaluation will be carried out and the comments and opinions of both parties will be recorded. A plan of development will be made and formal reviews will take place to check that targets are being met, with further comments and opinions being recorded. These reviews may be as often as every 3 months, but since this is a fairly time-consuming exercise, most reviews tend to be every 6 months.

Steps involved in appraisal process

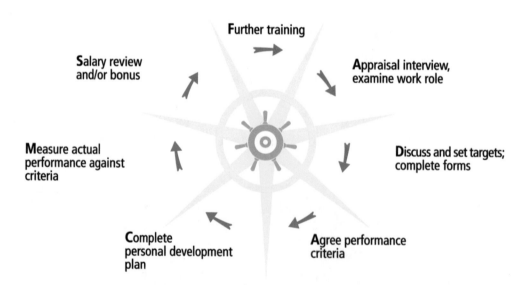

How is work performance evaluated?

This is the 'standard' of work that is expected from each employee. This can be very difficult to measure, but it can be done using a range of criteria, including:

- the ability to meet deadlines, return emails and phone calls and attend meetings
- the employee's monthly sales figures
- the number of complaints dealt with in a month by the employee
- the number of complaints made against the employee
- the employee's contribution to company profit.

Benefits of an appraisal system

- They let managers know what to expect from employees.
- They help managers develop skills in dealing with employees.
- They allow employees to discuss personal and professional development.
- They provide feedback to employees on their performance, and allow them to build on their strengths, eliminate weaknesses and increase productivity.
- They improve communication.
- They give the employee the opportunity of an 'open forum' when they can raise issues away from the workplace without having to worry about deadlines or their job.

There are problems associated with appraisals, however. Some managers conduct appraisal interviews very poorly. They do not allow enough time for the employee to discuss issues and they will avoid confrontation at all costs. They may not act on any issues discussed and the employee may be unwilling or afraid to take the matter further. Worse still, there may be no formal records of the meeting. This is sometimes referred to as a **closed** appraisal. The **open** appraisal may allow the employee to discuss issues and contribute to the records of the meeting but it does not guarantee that it will be a good appraisal. Employees themselves don't always tell the truth at appraisal interviews, usually because they want to avoid uncomfortable situations, direct confrontation, or being seen as a trouble maker. They don't want their honesty to hinder potential promotion.

Internet Research

Visit the website of the Chartered Institute of Personnel and Development for more information on appraisals, including fact sheets you can download.

Links to this site and other websites relating to Higher Administration can be found at: **www.leckieandleckie.co.uk** by clicking on the Learning Lab button and navigating to the Higher Administration Course Notes page.

Hint
Be prepared to discuss the benefits of the appraisal process and give reasons why appraisal is sometimes not successful.

Professional development

Staff development, or as it is known in some organisations, **continuing professional development** (CPD), allows staff to look at the job they are currently doing and identifying training or other activities which might help them to do it better.

> Staff development looks at what the employee needs to do to *enhance* their current skills, whereas an appraisal *measures* their existing ones.

Enhancing the skills that staff already have and linking their training and development to the strategic and operational plans of the organisation ensures that there is an efficient and fully qualified workforce. There also needs to be agreement on the evidence to be produced to prove that targets have been met. A product may be produced at the end of a course, or a further job role may be undertaken. Inducements such as bonuses or profit sharing schemes may also motivate staff.

Staff development will mean setting key objectives in agreement with the line manager. The starting point is the job/role description and the operational plan. Sometimes what is required is *education*, sometimes it is *development* and sometimes it is *training*. The difference between the three aspects is quite important as making sure that employees have core skills will allow greater flexibility when they transfer jobs.

- **Education:** the process of giving the employee the background academic knowledge to undertake the job (for example having a degree).
- **Training:** the process of gaining the knowledge and skills to do the current job.
- **Development:** the process of identifying future potential and undertaking either education or training to achieve it.

CPD – sometimes referred to as life-long learning – is seen as the most efficient and effective way of keeping staff motivated and up to date in this technology-driven and fast-changing economic and social environment. Governments actively encourage life-long learning. A strong commitment to CPD has advantages for the organisation as well as the individual employee: staff become more proficient at their jobs and customers are more satisfied; staff gain 'transferrable skills' allowing them to change jobs and to keep up with what is demanded from them, resulting in less stress and also being more adaptable to change. Most employers now recognise that education does not stop once an individual has gained employment and that they must allow staff time to pursue professional development activities, but the amount of time allowed for such activities varies from organisation to organisation.

Training

The main purpose of training is to improve performance. Most training starts with **induction**, the initial introduction to the organisation. After induction, training will be ongoing. Some organisations publish a list of courses and events that staff can attend. Some of these may be held within the organisation (in-house), others may be run off site (external).

Organisations work out which courses they need to offer by conducting a **training needs analysis** (or skills scan/audit) of their staff and the results of appraisals and development reviews. If an organisation is working towards, or has already achieved, Investors in People (IIP) status, then they will have a specific training policy.

IIP is a national quality standard based on three key principles covering 10 elements. In order to gain IIP status organisations are measured against these elements and UK businesses are encouraged to gain this award to demonstrate their commitment to providing a quality service. The assessment is rigorous and once awarded it is only valid for a 3 year period, after which time the organisation must be re-assessed and be awarded the standard again. (See page 66 for more information on IIP and management systems.)

Internet Research

Visit the IIP website to find out more about this quality standard. Download the brochure with information on the key principles, and make notes summarising the benefits of IIP status to an organisation.

Links to this site and other websites relating to Higher Administration can be found at: **www.leckieandleckie.co.uk** by clicking on the Learning Lab button and navigating to the Higher Administration Course Notes page.

Types of training

Balancing the training needs of a large organisation can be a complex process. Different people learn in different ways, and organisations need to consider this as they devise training courses – some employees will not attend courses (or will not benefit from them) if they are not appropriate to their needs.

Many trainers now adopt a **blended learning** approach, which is a mix of lecture, tutorial, practical activities and online materials to train staff. Some feel that the best way to learn is **on-the-job**. Different methods include:

- demonstrations
- job rotation (changing job roles every few months)
- coaching from a mentor
- working on a specific project – sometimes referred to as a **secondment**.

Off-the-job training includes:

- lectures
- online learning and distance/open learning
- case studies
- individual projects
- in-tray exercises.

The internet has helped in the development and use of training materials, and many employees are now encouraged to learn in their own time in places that suit them. As a result, many learning centres have been created within large organisations, for example, staff at Scottish Power have access to learning centres and electronic materials which they can work through in their own time as part of their CPD.

Hint
Can you explain 'blended learning'?

However, in-house and external training have both advantages and disadvantages.

In-house training

Advantages	Disadvantages
■ It can be tailored to suit specific requirements of the organisation ■ It is cheaper than external training ■ Employees do not need to travel long distances ■ It can be arranged to fit in with the other commitments of staff	■ Employees can sometimes be recalled from training if an emergency occurs ■ Training is not always taken seriously as staff may know the trainers ■ Course may be too specific for certain areas of the organisation

External training

Advantages	Disadvantages
■ Employees can meet and mix (network) with other colleagues ■ Employees can concentrate better away from the work environment ■ Employees are able to return to the workplace and pass on their knowledge to others (cascade) ■ It may be easier to introduce change ■ It may lead to a formally recognised qualification, for example, HNC	■ Can be expensive in terms of time and money ■ Employees may leave if they gain qualifications ■ Course may not always be relevant to the organisation ■ Employee may not pass the course assessments, costing more in terms of time and money

---

Quick Questions 2

1 List five aims of a successful appraisal.

2 Briefly describe the steps in the appraisal process.

3 Explain the differences between education, training and development.

4 Suggest why organisations may wish to gain the IIP standard.

5 List different types of learning methods used in *on-the-job* and *off-the-job* training.

Staff welfare

Employers are increasingly aware that a happy and healthy workforce will be more motivated and productive than one that is unhappy. Employers and Human Resource departments have to meet standards and conditions to comply with health and safety legislation, but some employers go beyond minimum requirements and have introduced even more staff-friendly schemes and policies. Many HR departments now have policies and procedures giving advice and information to staff.

Staff-friendly policies

Work–life balance: making sure that employees are able to spend time with their families and have time for recreation activities.

Employee well-being initiatives: introducing head massage, Pilates and healthy eating options to the organisation.

Time to talk: a counselling service where staff can speak in confidence.

Absence management: keeping track of how often and how long staff are absent for and the reasons they are absent. Providing 'back to work' interviews and an in-house doctor to check their progress and health.

Staff-friendly issues

More organisations are introducing employee well-being strategies or similar welfare initiatives to try and improve the physical and mental health of their workforce. The most common investment in employee well-being is in the provision of private health insurance, but along with counselling services many employers now provide 'stop-smoking' support for employees and some even provide subsidised gym memberships and exercise classes. Some organisations offer reflexology, yoga and meditation classes at lunchtime. Larger organisations may provide access to their own doctor, dentist or chiropodist (such as at large department stores).

Increasingly, employers are responding to their employees' demand for a more realistic work–life balance, and the need for individuals to have more control over when, where and how they work has led to an increasing demand for more flexible work patterns (see pages 22–23).

Internet Research

Visit Scotland's Health at Work website. Summarise the benefits of the programme. Look at the roll of honour to see which organisations in your area have gained awards.

Links to this site and other websites relating to Higher Administration can be found at: **www.leckieandleckie.co.uk** by clicking on the Learning Lab button and navigating to the Higher Administration Course Notes page.

Counselling

Many employees suffer from **stress**. Stress may be related to work or personal issues (family or health) but anything that affects an employee's work performance needs to be addressed. Stress may lead to the employee not sleeping well, drinking or smoking too much, being over-anxious and/or argumentative. This can affect their concentration and judgement, resulting in them being unable to cope with their work. Some organisations provide access to external counselling services and encourage their employees to speak to a counsellor about their problems. Counsellors help with personal problems, for example a death in the family or marital problems, as well as work and health problems. All matters are treated in the strictest confidence and no records are kept in employee files.

Internet Research

Visit the BUPA website and look at the fact sheet on Stress in the workplace. Note the causes, triggers and effects of stress, and how to avoid them.

Links to this site and other websites relating to Higher Administration can be found at: **www.leckieandleckie.co.uk** by clicking on the Learning Lab button and navigating to the Higher Administration Course Notes page.

Advice on grievance and disciplinary procedures

To ensure that all employees are treated fairly HR departments must make sure that they have clear procedures to deal with discipline and grievance. Details of these may be provided with the contract of employment. Disciplinary procedures have already been mentioned on pages 28–29. Grievances, however, are raised by employees when they are unhappy about how they have been treated or about something that has happened at work, such as:

- they think they have been demoted or have less pay than expected
- there has been a change in the physical environment or job conditions
- they feel that they are being sexually harassed or bullied.

It is important to have a **grievance procedure** so that all issues are dealt with fairly and quickly. It also acts as a guide to all those involved in the actual process. In the first instance it is a good idea to try and deal with any complaints and grievances informally, as this is more cost-effective and less time consuming. It also leaves less time for a grievance to fester and helps maintain better relationships between an employee and their line manager or organisation.

A grievance procedure should:

- make it easy for an employee to raise issues with management
- be available in writing and simple to understand
- enable a line manager to deal informally with a grievance
- keep proceedings confidential
- allow the employee to have a companion at any formal grievance meeting/hearing.

"...and Maureen from accounts would like a softer chair..."

Steps in the procedure are:

- **step 1:** inform the line manager of the grievance in writing
- **step 2:** meet with the manager to discuss the grievance with a representative if necessary
- **step 3:** if the matter is not resolved meet with a more senior manager
- **step 4:** be given the right to an appeal meeting if the employee feels that a grievance has not been satisfactorily resolved and be notified of the final decision.

Grievances should take place within set time limits; depending on the seriousness of the grievance this could be within a few days or a week of the grievance being lodged. If there is no agreed resolution then matters can be taken to the Advice, Conciliation and Arbitration Service (ACAS) to settle.

Internet Research

Visit the ACAS website and search the site for information on handling grievances. Make notes on the advantages to employee and employer of clear grievance procedures.

Links to this site and other websites relating to Higher Administration can be found at: **www.leckieandleckie.co.uk** by clicking on the Learning Lab button and navigating to the Higher Administration Course Notes page.

Procedures for dealing with absence and illness

Procedures for dealing with absence and illness will vary between organisations. An organisation cannot afford to ignore either short-term or long-term absences, because consequences can include:

- loss of productivity and increased costs
- additional work for the remaining staff – people covering for absent staff never know all of their colleague's job role, causing additional problems
- repeated absences can cause resentment in the workforce.

To address such problems many HR departments have put procedures in place to address absence, while making sure that they are still sensitive to the individual concerned. Such procedures include:

- keeping in contact with the individual while they are absent from work
- arranging return-to-work interviews
- agree staged return-to-work which may mean reduced hours and a change in work for a period of time
- arranging for the employee to meet with the organisation's doctor
- using disciplinary procedures if appropriate for short-term absences
- involvement of occupational health professionals and rehabilitation programmes if it is long-term absence.

An employee's return to work must be managed and planned – support must be given from line managers and the HR department so that the employee is treated fairly and receives benefits in line with employment legislation.

Quick Questions 3

1 List four effects of stress on an employee's work performance.
2 Give reasons why it is better to solve a grievance informally.
3 State the purpose of ACAS.
4 Outline the procedures that may be used to manage continual short-term absences.
5 Explain why an organisation may offer access to sports facilities for its staff.

Extended Response Questions

1 *Justify* an organisation's decision to recruit for a new post internally. [6 marks]

2 *Discuss* the **consequences** of poor interview preparation to both the interviewer and the interviewee. [8 marks]

3 *Describe* the benefits of an appraisal system to both the employer and the employee. [6 marks]

4 *Compare* the different forms of external training available for staff development. [8 marks]

5 Staff absence and illness costs money. *Discuss* how an absence management system can reduce costs and decrease the time lost through absence. [10 marks]

6 *Describe*, giving examples, what you understand by the term 'work–life balance'. [6 marks]

4 MEETINGS

Meetings

Meetings take place in all organisations. If run poorly, meetings can be boring and/or a waste of time. However, meetings are necessary in order to communicate information to a number of people at the same time. The main purposes of meetings are:

- to discuss and generate ideas
- to consult on issues and problem solve
- to motivate and for team building
- to set targets and objectives
- to plan and make decisions.

Effective meetings

1 Plan the meeting first – is it absolutely necessary?
2 Make sure it has a clear purpose.   ] planning
3 Prepare an agenda and circulate before the meeting.
4 Set a time limit for the meeting to last, for example, 1 hour.   ] control
5 Delegate responsibilities, keep control and agree outcomes and actions.
6 Follow up on agreed actions.

Meetings range from the very informal chat by the water-cooler, where an exchange of information is sometimes known as the 'office grapevine' (due to the speed at which such information is passed around the office), to the organisation's very formal annual general meeting.

The formality of a meeting is usually determined by how it is conducted. If an agenda has been sent out, proper meeting terminology used and there are recognised office bearers like a chairperson, secretary, treasurer and minutes taker, then this will be a formal meeting. However, if the meeting is for a team or section, it may be less formal – there may still be an agenda, but instead of full minutes being taken only action minutes may be recorded. This is the most common type of meeting and is used to team build and keep staff informed.

Formal meetings need to follow rules laid down by the organisation's **articles of association**. If it is a club these rules are called the **constitution** and in local authorities they are called **standing orders**. The rules generally state that:

- before a meeting can take place proper notice must be given to allow all those who wish to attend to do so
- the chairperson needs to be present
- a minimum number (quorum) of attendees must be present
- the main office bearers are present
- the meeting is conducted as laid down in the articles of association, constitution or standing orders.

Annual general meeting

By law, all public limited companies must hold an **annual general meeting** (AGM). As the name implies, it must take place once each year, and all shareholders are invited to it. The regulations stating how the meeting should be conducted are laid down in the Companies Acts.

The purposes of an AGM are:

- to discuss the performance of the company over the year and examine the accounts and balance sheet of the organisation
- to accept the directors' and auditors' reports
- to elect new office bearers
- to agree the dividend to be paid to shareholders.

Extraordinary general meeting

This is another very formal meeting that must follow the procedural regulations laid down by the Companies Acts. It is open to all shareholders or members and is usually held to resolve or discuss some issue that cannot wait until the AGM – for example, a financial crisis.

Board meeting

Limited companies are usually run by a **board of directors**, who hold regular meetings to discuss the strategic aims of the organisation and its policies. If it is necessary to concentrate on certain aspects of the business, the board may recommend the delegation of duties and tasks to be carried out by committees set up for that purpose.

Types of committee

- **Executive:** tends to be set up to make decisions that are binding, for example, issues regarding equal opportunities.
- **Advisory:** to give advice on a specific issue, for example, on relocating to an out-of-town site.
- **Joint:** set up to improve communications between two separate committees, for example, Staff Social Committee and Staff Welfare Committee.
- **Standing:** is in permanent existence to deal with a specific remit, for example, health and safety.
- **Ad hoc:** this is formed only for a particular issue or task, for example, to arrange a special event like a retiral (someone leaving because they have reached retirement age) or the opening of new premises. The committee will be disbanded once the event is finished.
- **Sub-committee:** this is a standing or ad hoc committee formed out of one of the above, for example, an Equal Opportunities Committee may decide to form a sub-committee to investigate ageism in the organisation.

The chairperson

The **chairperson** must have personal skills and qualities to control the meeting. They need to be respected by all the other members and will need to show tact and diplomacy when dealing with the issues. They will also need to be fair in their judgements and use their casting vote wisely (see page 54 about casting votes).

The chairperson is responsible for:

- compiling the agenda
- ensuring that the previous minutes are correct
- ensuring there is a minimum number of people present to start the meeting (a quorum)
- starting and ending the meeting on time
- keeping control of the meeting
- making sure everyone who wishes to speak gets the opportunity to do so
- explaining complex issues
- deciding when it is time to vote, and summarising the discussion
- declaring the results of the vote and recording the results
- making decisions
- closing or adjourning the meeting formally.

After the meeting the chairperson will

- liaise with the secretary regarding the preparation of the draft minutes and the agenda for the next meeting.
- take follow-up actions from the discussions as required
- make any necessary decisions between meetings, usually in consultation with the secretary.

Hint

You will not be asked an exam question covering all aspects of meetings. Sometimes the question also relates meetings to other parts of the syllabus. For example, a question may ask about health and safety, or consumer groups and meetings at the same time. Remember: meetings are held by all types of bodies and organisations.

The secretary

Organising a meeting requires administrative support and there are duties which the secretary needs to perform before, during and after the meeting. Whether it is an AGM or a team meeting affects how much work needs to be done.

Before the meeting

- Book the venue – whether it is for a large conference or a team meeting, this is one of the first things to do. Always allow a little time before and after the meeting to get the room organised and cleared up.
- Make sure that the room is laid out appropriately, for example, one large table and chairs (particularly useful if attendees have lots of papers) or just chairs. Alternatively, more than one room may be required if you are going to have working groups.

- Order refreshments, making sure that special dietary requirements are catered for and always include water. Indicate when refreshments are to be available.
- Book any equipment that may be needed, for example, a data projector and laptop if a presentation is to be given, or a DVD player if a programme is to be shown.
- Inform reception where the meeting is taking place and arrange for parking spaces/permits if necessary. Ensure that there is disabled access.
- Make a note in appropriate diaries, including the chairperson's diary, regarding the date, time and the place.
- Make extra copies of the agenda and minutes of the last meeting to bring to the meeting.
- Make a note of any apologies received.
- Prepare name badges for the attendees.
- Inform the press if the meeting is a public one and is likely to be reported.

On the day of the meeting
- Inform reception where the meeting is being held and give the names of those expected to attend.
- Check the room is as expected and that refreshments are ordered and that the heating, lighting and seating are in order.
- Check that the equipment requested has arrived and is working.
- Make sure that there are signs or directions to the meeting room.
- Place a 'Meeting in progress' sign on the door.
- Prepare the attendance register.
- Be in the room ready to greet the attendees.

During the meeting
- Sit next to the chairperson so that you can pass them any relevant papers and assist them throughout the meeting.
- Read the minutes and any apologies received if required.
- Make sure the chairperson signs the minutes and signs any alterations.
- Ensure everyone signs the attendance register.
- Take notes for the minutes of the meeting and make sure that they include what has to be done, by whom, and when.
- Make a separate note for any actions required by the chairperson.
- Distribute any expense claim forms.

After the meeting
- Tidy the room and collect all unused papers. Inform reception, switchboard and catering that the meeting is finished.
- Draft out the minutes from the notes taken as soon as possible and give a copy to the chairperson.
- Make a note in your diary of when the agenda for the next meeting should be prepared and send it out with a copy of the minutes.
- Follow up any actions from the meeting.
- Write any letters as required from the meeting.

- Make a note of the date of the next meeting.
- Contact attendees who have actions from the meeting to check that they are comfortable with what they have to do.
- When necessary prepare the agenda and chairperson's agenda for the next meeting (see pages 50–52).

Hint

It is unlikely that you will be asked a straightforward question regarding the duties *before*, *during* and *after* a meeting. However, you may be asked the role of the secretary or chairperson with regards to these duties. Alternatively you may be asked about the *consequences* of not making adequate preparation for meetings, or to *compare* the roles of different office bearers.

Quick Questions 1

1 List the main reasons for holding a meeting.
2 Explain the term 'office grapevine'. What role does it play in an organisation?
3 Identify three different types of committee meeting.
4 Outline the role of the chairperson at a meeting.
5 List the steps that can be taken to control meetings.

Consequences of poorly planned meetings

Organising a meeting may seem like an awful lot of work – and it is – but if it is done properly things will run smoothly and efficiently. When a meeting has not been well organised it reflects on the organisation and the person responsible for organising the meeting.

Consequences of poor meeting organisation

- The meeting may be postponed, particularly if attendees have not received the meeting papers or the agenda with sufficient notice.
- A badly designed agenda may lead to time wasting and the meeting taking longer than necessary.
- If attendees have not received the minutes or papers for the meeting in sufficient time they might not have time to read them, so might not be able to join the discussion effectively.
- Attendees may be made to feel uncomfortable if refreshments do not include water – not everyone will drink tea or coffee.
- An attendee may be embarrassed, or even angry, if the food provided does not include a vegetarian option.
- If reception has not been informed of a meeting they may misdirect attendees and make them late for the meeting.
- If parking has not been arranged, or if there is no disabled access, it may result in attendees being late (and annoyed).
- If the correct meeting procedures have not been followed then any decisions taken at the meeting could be invalid.

Internet Research

Visit the Effective Meetings website. Make notes of the summary at the bottom of the page. Follow the related link on creating an agenda. Read the information and take any notes that might be useful.

Links to this site and other websites relating to Higher Administration can be found at: **www.leckieandleckie.co.uk** by clicking on the Learning Lab button and navigating to the Higher Administration Course Notes page.

Documentation relating to meetings

Notice of meeting and agenda

Information regarding the **notice of the meeting** is usually combined with the **agenda**. This document is usually sent some time before the meeting to give the attendees an opportunity to prepare for the meeting. Normally, no more than 2 weeks' notice is given as people can forget if a meeting is too far in advance. If the meeting is formal the secretary will usually sign the notice of meeting.

NOTICE OF MEETING

A meeting of the Equal Opportunities Committee will be held in the Conference Suite, on **Thursday 8 May 2008** at **3 pm**.

AGENDA

1	Apologies for absence
2	Minutes of previous meeting
3	Matters arising
4	New Equalities Act
5	Ramp and doors at the emergency exit
6	Any other business
7	Date of next meeting

standard items

Eilidh McLean
Secretary

1 May 2008

Hint

Some of the items in the agenda are standard – they will appear in every agenda. Usually they are the first three (apologies, minutes of previous meeting, and matters arising) and the last two items (any other business and date of next meeting).

Formal minutes of a meeting

Minutes are the official record of the meeting and are usually taken by the secretary. The minutes are normally written in the past tense and third person (for example, *Christen Marr reported on the positive feedback received from the IIP inspection*). A record is not made of everything that was said at the meeting, but details of the proposals and resolutions are noted. A record is also made of proposers and seconders of motions, any decisions that are made and of any actions that need to be taken (with details of who is responsible, and when the action should be completed by). The minutes are usually recorded in the same order as the items appear on the agenda. Once the meeting has agreed that the minutes from the previous meeting are a correct record of what was discussed they are usually signed by the chairperson and filed in the minute book.

MINUTES OF MEETING

Minutes of the Equal Opportunities Committee meeting held in the Conference Suite on Thursday 8 May 2008 at 3 pm.

PRESENT
Niall Anderson (Chair); Eilidh McLean (secretary); Helen Mack; Christen Marr; Emma Nolan; Sopita Patak; Frank Thomson

1   APOLOGIES FOR ABSENCE
Apologies were received from Catriona Mayhew and Andrew Cash.

2   MINUTES OF THE PREVIOUS MEETING
The minutes of the previous meeting were taken as read, agreed and signed by the chairperson.

3   MATTERS ARISING
Staff had requested an information session regarding the implementation of the new Equalities Act. This had become law in April and was on the agenda to be discussed.

4   NEW EQUALITIES ACT
The purpose of this new Act was discussed at length, i.e. all public authorities in Great Britain must demonstrate that they are promoting equality for women and men and that they are eliminating sexual discrimination and harassment. The Gender Equality Duty will bring about real change in the culture of organisations as the onus will be on organisations to promote equality, rather than on individuals to highlight discrimination. Christen proposed a presentation should be given to staff at the end of the month by members of the Committee. This was seconded by Frank and carried.

5   RAMP AND DOORS AT THE EMERGENCY EXIT
Access to the emergency exit is currently under review as there have been a number of complaints about difficulties with the doors. It was agreed that Helen Mack should speak to Technical Support to investigate what was causing the problem and report back at the next meeting.

6   ANY OTHER BUSINESS
Sopita suggested that a sub-committee would need to be set up to organise the Retiral Dinner for Andrew Cash in July. It was agreed that Sopita, Eilidh and Emma could deal with this.

7   DATE OF NEXT MEETING
It was agreed that the next meeting would be held on 16 July at 3 pm.

Eilidh McLean   Date: 14 May 2008

Action minutes

With the increased use of email and other technologies and a constant drive to be more efficient, less formal meetings now tend to adopt the **action minutes** approach. Action minutes do not record as much information as formal minutes but tend to concentrate on three key areas:

- what has to be done
- who is responsible for doing it
- when it has to be done by.

Many organisations have their own house style for action minutes, but the following layout is fairly typical.

TEAM MEETING ACTION POINTS

Notes from the meeting of the Equal Opportunities Committee held in the Conference Suite on Thursday 8 May 2008 at 3 pm.

PRESENT: Niall, Eilidh, Helen, Christen, Emma, Sopita and Frank

APOLOGIES: Catriona and Andrew

TOPIC	ACTION	DEADLINE	INITIALS
New Equalities Act Give presentation to staff at the end of the month	Prepare presentation	31 May	CM
Ramp and Door at Emergency Exit Problems with the doors	Speak to Technical Support	By next meeting	HM
AOB Retiral Dinner for Andrew Cash	Set up sub-committee	ASAP	EM, EN, SP

Chairperson's agenda

Sometimes a separate chairperson's agenda will be prepared. A chairperson's agenda is most often used in a formal meeting or if the chairperson is new to the job. It is basically the same as a normal agenda with space on the right-hand side of the sheet for the chairperson to make notes as the meeting progresses.

CHAIRPERSON'S AGENDA

AGENDA ITEM	NOTES
1 Apologies for absence	*No apology received from Mark*
2 Matters arising	*Remember to mention the new canteen manager*
3 New Equalities Act	*Suggest staff access website www.eoc.org.uk*

Internet Research

Visit the Secretarial Site website. Follow the links to Agendas, Meetings and Minutes to get different views on the documentation associated with meetings.

Links to this site and other websites relating to Higher Administration can be found at: **www.leckieandleckie.co.uk** by clicking on the Learning Lab button and navigating to the Higher Administration Course Notes page.

Quick Questions 2

1 Describe why you think agendas and minutes are used when holding meetings.
2 List the factors to take into account when booking refreshments for a meeting.
3 Outline the standard items that will be found on most agendas.
4 Explain the difference between action minutes and formal minutes.
5 Who is responsible for setting the agenda for a meeting?

Meeting terminology

Although some people regard the terminology used for meetings as 'jargon', if a formal meeting is taking place many of these terms will be found in the agenda or minutes and used during the meetings, so you need to know what they mean. The following list contains some of the terms used during and about meetings.

Abstain
When a vote is taken on a motion, if a person neither votes for nor against then they *abstain*.

Address the Chair
At a formal meeting if a member wishes to speak then they must first of all say 'Madame Chairperson'/ 'Mr Chairman' before saying their piece. This prevents more than one person talking at the same time.

Adjournment
This is when a meeting has to be stopped because it has run out of time, but will be resumed at a later date, or if more information is needed before a discussion can continue.

Amendment
If there is to be a change to a proposed *motion* then this is said to be an amendment. It might include the addition/deletion or insertion of words and it has to be *proposed*, *seconded* and voted upon in the usual way.

Ballot
This is the process of voting. Sometimes it might simply be a show of hands, but on other occasions it might be a secret ballot, in which case the votes will be put in a sealed box and counted.

Casting vote

If there are an equal number of votes for and against a *motion* then the chairperson will have an 'extra vote' so that a decision can be made.

Majority

This is when more than half of the people at the meeting vote for or against a motion.

Motion

This is a proposal to take forward the discussion to a vote. It requires a *proposer* and a *seconder*. It is discussed and before the vote is taken the *proposer* has the 'right of reply' which allows them to make a final comment after all the discussion has taken place.

Point of order

This is a query regarding procedures or the way the meeting is being conducted.

Postpone

If a meeting cannot take place due to unforeseen circumstances then it may be put off to a later date. If the discussion of an item is put off to another meeting this is a postponement too.

Proposer

This is the person who puts forward a *motion* for discussion at a meeting.

Quorum

This is the minimum number of people who need to attend a meeting to make it legal.

Resolution

Once a *motion* has been passed it becomes a resolution.

Seconder

This is the person who supports the person who proposes a *motion*.

Standing orders

These are the rules and regulations which an organisation must follow; they detail how meetings have to be conducted.

Unanimous

This when everyone votes the same way for or against a *motion*.

Verbatim

This means 'word for word'. Sometimes when it is very important that a minute is recorded exactly it might be verbatim.

Internet Research

Use a search engine such as Google, AltaVista or Yahoo, or the online encyclopedia Wikipedia and search for the meaning of the following terms related to meetings:

- no confidence
- proxy vote
- *ex officio*

- rider
- in camera
- lie on the table

- *ad hoc*
- *sine die*
- *sederunt*

Links to this site and other websites relating to Higher Administration can be found at: **www.leckieandleckie.co.uk** by clicking on the Learning Lab button and navigating to the Higher Administration Course Notes page.

Hint

You need to be familiar with the meeting terminology, especially the words on pages 53–54.
Make sure that you know the meanings of each of the words.

ICT has had a huge impact on the way that meetings are now conducted. There are now various tools which will facilitate both the organising and running of meetings.

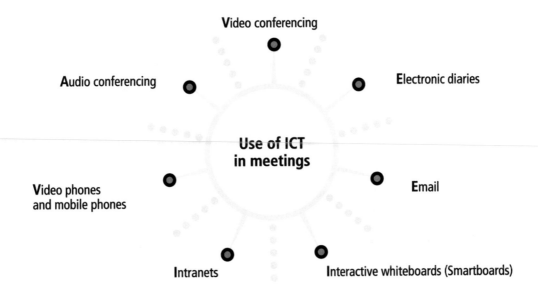

In the past, the amount of paper that was used in preparing for meetings used to be described as 'cutting down a forest'. First, the people invited to the meeting had to be sent a notice of meeting and agenda. Next the minutes had to be copied and sent out. In addition, any papers that the minutes referred to would also have to be copied and enclosed. If people were travelling to the meeting from other parts of the country or world then arrangements had to be made for accommodation and travel, which meant expense claims had to be prepared. Extra copies of the minutes and agenda were usually made in case people forgot to bring them to the meeting. Sometimes trying to arrange a meeting was also difficult as phoning did not always get the person required and it might take a few days before finding out if they could attend or not. However, ICT has changed all that and the most common tools used now include:

- electronic diaries
- email
- intranets
- audio conferencing
- video conferencing
- video phones
- mobiles phone
- interactive whiteboards
- internet and network meetings

Electronic diaries

These are particularly useful for setting up meetings as long as the secretary has access to everyone's diary. The secretary can look in the required e-diaries and check for a free date and time, so can arrange a meeting much more quickly. Once the secretary invites people to attend the meeting, electronic diaries will be updated automatically when the attendee accepts the invitation. Some e-diaries will also send reminders (a day or other specified time interval before the meeting) to the attendee's email. The secretary can use the e-diary to be reminded of key dates, for example, when to chase confirmation of the room booking or when certain items need to be sent out.

Email

This facilitates the sending of attachments along with the notice of meeting and agenda to multiple recipients all at the same time. It means that there is no need for paper copies – saving all those trees! If someone forgets their copy at the meeting it may be possible to refer to the document on a laptop screen as the electronic file can be easily accessed and opened. The electronic storage of documentation is simple and does not use up as much space as physical paper copies.

Intranets

Many companies have their own intranets which are really just private networks. Increasingly, companies are using them for storing policies and procedures, forms and templates. Staff can access an intranet any time they are logged on to the network. The potential benefit of this is that the forms and policies that are held centrally (on the intranet) should be the most up-to-date ones, so there is less chance of staff using an out-of-date version of something. Minutes of previous meetings can also be stored on the intranet so staff can access them at any time.

Audio conferencing

This is usually conducted by telephones on loud speaker, where a group of people sit around a telephone, communicating with other groups of people in other locations doing the same thing. One of the main drawbacks of holding a meeting in this way is that it is not always easy to identify the person speaking unless they give their name before talking. Another problem is that it is not possible to see the facial expressions or body language of those at other locations so it might be difficult to know how they really feel about something or what they really mean. It is not a very good method to use if a conversation is confidential. However, it can be quite a successful way of holding a brief meeting between a few people.

Video conferencing

This method of communication has revolutionised the way meetings are now held. Nearly all large organisations have video conferencing facilities; these usually consist of a large television/plasma screen, a computer network and video conferencing software. The facilities must be available at all organisations taking part in the video conference. The link allows two or more groups of people in different parts of the country (or even the world) to meet and discuss business without having the problems of travel and accommodation. This saves an enormous amount of time and money and it has been very successful in improving communication in large multinational companies. Companies that do not have video conferencing facilities can hire the service from another company or supplier.

Advantages of video conferencing

- Ability to communicate with other people over long distances (with the added advantage of being able to see and hear what they are saying and respond to body language).
- It is more personal than a telephone call.
- There is less need for people to travel, which saves money and helps the environment by cutting down on pollution from cars and other non-environmentally friendly forms of transport.
- It saves staff time as the video conference facility will be either in or close to their normal place of work.
- Meetings can be recorded and played back.
- Allows for demonstrations and the use of visual aids.

Disadvantages of video conferencing

- The hardware and software needed for a top-end video conferencing system can be very expensive.
- Time differences can be a problem with international meetings.
- Integrated Services Digital Network (ISDN) lines are needed, which are expensive to set up and use. An alternative is to use broadband connections.
- If there is a network fault or the system crashes, the meeting will have to be postponed or delayed, which may cause frustration.
- Participants may feel awkward being filmed.

Video phones

These are just telephones with a screen, so are helpful if you want to see the person you are talking to. Sometimes they are used instead of video conferencing as they are cheaper. However, only one or two people can take part in a meeting using this method. Sometimes video phones are used in television news reports, when reporters give stories from remote areas.

Mobile phones

Mobile phones have become essential tools for keeping in touch with colleagues and friends, but perhaps their biggest influence has been in the growth of 'text messaging'. This is now one of the most common methods of communication, but it may encourage poor spelling, and may have a negative effect on the use of proper business language as some employees use text language in email messages.

Mobile phones can allow the user to send and receive calls and messages, store messages, use voicemail, take and receive pictures and small movies, surf the internet and download music and games. They are invaluable for the business person who has to travel away from the office regularly as they can be used almost anywhere (although some areas have poor or no reception).

Unfortunately, many people forget to turn off their phones in meetings and in public places like theatres and cinemas. Many organisations now have a mobile phone policy which usually states that the mobile should be on silent or vibrate modes and that personal calls should not be made or received during working hours.

Interactive whiteboards

These are a 'virtual' electronic version of a flip chart or whiteboard. They are typically used to lecture or give presentations and allow the user to write or draw over a presentation that is being projected on the board. They are also sensitive to touch so sometimes by just touching the board with a finger the operator can open a new file or access information stored on a laptop. The biggest advantage of using an interactive whiteboard in a meeting is that it can all be saved electronically, for example, if a brainstorming session has taken place the notes can be easily saved, printed out or emailed to participants later.

Internet and network meetings

Most organisations will either use a local area network (LAN) or wide area network (WAN) to connect computers, communicate and share resources. This means that there are even more tools available to communicate with and therefore use to contribute to virtual meetings. These tools are:

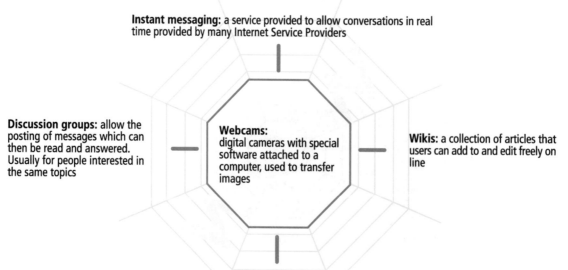

Instant messaging: a service provided to allow conversations in real time provided by many Internet Service Providers

Discussion groups: allow the posting of messages which can then be read and answered. Usually for people interested in the same topics

Webcams: digital cameras with special software attached to a computer, used to transfer images

Wikis: a collection of articles that users can add to and edit freely on line

Blogs: online diaries where thoughts or opinions can be displayed

Note: See Chapter 7 for more information on the impact of ICT on work practices.

Hint

Make sure you can give specific examples of how ICT has improved the efficiency of meetings.

Quick Questions 3

1 What is the importance of a quorum to a meeting?
2 Outline the stages of a motion at a meeting.
3 Explain the purpose of a casting vote.
4 Compare the use of paper diaries and electronic diaries when arranging meetings.
5 State how the use of networks has facilitated electronic communication, especially in relation to meetings.

1 The board of directors has set up an ad hoc committee to examine the problems caused by the difficulties in parking and the lack of parking spaces.
   Explain the meaning of the term 'ad hoc' and ***describe*** three other types of committee meeting. [8 marks]

2 ***Compare*** the factors that would need to be considered when booking an external as opposed to an internal venue for a meeting. [6 marks]

3 ***Justify*** the importance of producing minutes of a formal meeting. [4 marks]

4 ***Outline*** the possible ***consequences*** of inadequate preparation for holding a meeting by video conferencing. [4 marks]

5 ***Identify*** and ***describe*** the main qualities and skills required by a chairperson. [6 marks]

6 ***Discuss*** the different uses and advantages of ICT when arranging and holding meetings. [8 marks]

Customer service policies

Today most organisations make a commitment to their customers to provide the best possible service in the most efficient way at the best price. They usually have a **mission statement** which outlines the organisation's main aims and goals. This statement is usually only a couple of sentences but employees are encouraged to learn it and share the management's 'vision' of how the organisation hopes to grow and develop.

> Customer service is probably the most important aspect of any business, as without customers there is no business!

Because of increased global competition the market place is now extremely competitive and attracting and retaining customers is a prime factor in many customer service policies.

In order to meet increased customer expectations businesses need to implement procedures that ensure customer satisfaction. Satisfied customers will be happy customers who will tend to come back and even recommend the organisation to others.

Customers are not only external to the organisation but are also internal (employees and stakeholders). If the staff are motivated and valued they will be more likely to promote a good company image. Even the way the telephone is answered can have an effect on a potential customer. Therefore it is important to be professional at all times. To encourage such professionalism, many organisations will have a **customer care/service strategy** in place which will be a written statement of principles to ensure that the customer gets what they *want* at the *right standard*, *quality* and *price*. In addition, the strategy will outline the organisation's policy regarding how it will:

Customer is King

- ensure the quality of its customer care
- measure and test that customer needs are satisfied
- ensure service level agreements are in place
- deal with customer complaints.

Poor customer care will result in dissatisfied customers and a high level of complaints. This may lead to a bad reputation which is always very difficult to win back.

In terms of providing effective customer care, the administrative assistant should:

- **be competent:** establish a professional and knowledgeable image, and treat the customer courteously, using their names if possible, for example, Mr Brown or Ms Varsi
- **be confident:** keep good eye contact and smile at the customer; positive body language is important

- **be concerned:** listen attentively to what the customer has to say, and be honest even if you have to give bad news, as gaining a customer's trust helps customer relations
- **be courteous:** be polite and don't argue with a customer, even if they are shouting or being abusive – be assertive but not aggressive
- **communicate:** ask questions, take notes, pass on information and keep the customer informed.

Internet Research

Using a search engine of your choice find the mission statements of the following companies: McDonald's, Marks & Spencer and Sainsbury's plc. Write each one out and note any similarities.

Links to these sites and other websites relating to Higher Administration can be found at: **www.leckieandleckie.co.uk** by clicking on the Learning Lab button and navigating to the Higher Administration Course Notes page.

Customer care strategy

This is a statement about the standards that a customer can expect from an organisation. If the organisation produces a good or service that no one else does or they are a very large organisation, they can reduce prices against their competitors and may worry less about their standards in customer care because of the strength they have in the market place. However, customers always have a choice and they may choose not to use or buy from a particular organisation if they are dissatisfied.

A good customer care strategy will allow an organisation to benefit from:

- achieving customer satisfaction
- increased sales
- increased customer loyalty
- a good reputation
- increased competitiveness
- fewer complaints.

Customer service level agreement

This is basically an agreement between the organisation and the customer describing what the organisation promises to be able to do and what the customer can expect. It will be a clear, detailed policy that:

- states what, how and when the organisation intends to deliver
- states what happens if the organisation fails in its promise and commitment
- outlines the responsibilities of both parties
- specifies any extra or hidden costs.

Its main purpose is to increase customer confidence and therefore encourage the customer to use the organisation, but it also helps the organisation to establish standards against which they can measure themselves and compare with other organisations.

"I really must tell Joe about this place"

"I'm never coming back here again!"

Benefits of good customer service	Effects of poor customer service
■ Motivated and high performing staff	■ Demoralised and demotivated staff
■ Satisfied and loyal customers who return to the organisation and recommend it to friends	■ Dissatisfied customers will not return and will not recommend the organisation, resulting in loss of income
■ Good reputation which will attract both customers and new staff	■ It is extremely difficult to turn around a poor reputation – think of Gerald Ratner and his comment about 'cheap jewellery' – his shops disappeared from the high street!
■ Competitive edge in the market place	■ Lose standing and status in the market place
■ Increased market share	■ May need to downsize and/or increase spending on advertising and changing image

Remember

- Survival depends on the customer.
- Repeat customers are important customers.
- Satisfaction is essential.
- Satisfaction depends on high quality.
- Satisfaction depends on continual improvement.

Complaints procedures

Most organisations will have procedures to deal with any complaints. In some cases there may be a specific complaints department. It is important that both staff and customers know how to use the procedures. Although a lot of people do complain, it is acknowledged that some customers will accept bad service and will not complain. However, they may not return to the organisation and they will tell their friends and colleagues of their bad experiences.

Complaints

- All complaints should be treated seriously and logged.
- They should be handled by specially trained staff.
- They should be acknowledged and the customer should be kept informed of what is happening.
- Time limits for dealing with complaints should be established, for example, all complaints will be dealt with in 10 working days.
- The result of the investigation into the complaint should be communicated to the customer promptly.

Reasons given by customers for not complaining are shown in the diagram.

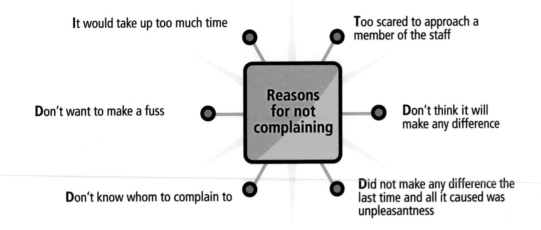

○——— Quick Questions 1 ———○

1 Explain the difference between a 'vision' and a 'mission statement'.
2 Outline the purpose of an organisation's customer care strategy.
3 List three benefits to an organisation of having an effective customer care strategy.
4 Identify the main qualities of an administrative assistant working in customer care.
5 State the consequences to an organisation of poor customer service.

Methods of evaluating policy

Having a way to evaluate customer care policy allows an organisation to:

- monitor where complaints come from and what they are about
- target where training or changes in procedures need to be introduced
- assure customers of prompt attention at all times
- show commitment to customers, encouraging their loyalty and gaining their trust and respect.

Organisations that show a willingness to find and eliminate customer problems will achieve a **customer focus**.

How to improve customer focus

- Listen to what the customers have to say – share feedback and information.
- Conduct focus groups to find out what they like/dislike and what improvements they recommend.
- Develop a customer satisfaction survey to send out to all the customers.
- Create a 'Best Customer Service Awards' board to publicly recognise the 'Best Staff Member' for the month.
- Provide special customer service training.
- Create an internal newsletter that shares good practice around the whole organisation.
- Provide warranties, guarantees and refunds.

Guarantees and warranties

A **guarantee** is a formal promise by an organisation and it represents the organisation's own belief in the quality of its products. Companies that offer a 'money-back' guarantee know that a small number of people will ask for their money back but in general this policy will bring in more business. A **warranty** assures the customer that the organisation is stating that their goods or service will last for an appropriate length of time, but if the need arises the customer may get repairs or replacements at no extra cost. However, organisations must ensure that they clearly explain the terms of their guarantees and warranties to avoid any later disputes.

Internet Research

Search the websites of the following organisations:

- the Office of Fair Trading – find out how to avoid scams and try the Scambusters quiz
- Consumer Direct – find out how the law protects your rights
- Trading Standards Organisation – look for advice leaflets for consumers, and try to find out how many products have been recalled in the last week.

Links to these sites and other websites relating to Higher Administration can be found at: **www.leckieandleckie.co.uk** by clicking on the Learning Lab button and navigating to the Higher Administration Course Notes page.

Surveying customer satisfaction

Listening to customers means finding out what they are saying and there are various ways of collecting the information required, including:

- questionnaires
- comment cards
- telephone interviews
- interviews in the street
- online surveys.

The most formal method is the **questionnaire**. However, not everyone likes filling in questionnaires, so an incentive like entry into a prize draw or a free gift is often given to encourage customers to complete questionnaires. These questionnaires or written surveys provide permanent records of what customers feel and the results can be analysed for statistical purposes.

Customer feedback can also be collected by **comment cards** put in suggestion boxes. Unfortunately, some people don't take these seriously and some suggestions are not always entirely appropriate.

Customers may be **telephoned** to find out their opinions. This method can cheaply and effectively be outsourced to call centres, but some customers resent being interrupted at home, especially as many calls are made between 5.30 pm and 7.30 pm to get people at home after work.

Occasionally, organisations employ people to stop customers in the street to **interview** them on a one-to-one basis to find out their opinions on products and services. This is a time-consuming and expensive process, and it can be unpleasant if people are rude.

Increasingly, **online surveys** are being used as people find it quick and simple to complete online forms; however, they don't always read the questions properly, so may not provide accurate information.

Loyalty cards

Loyalty cards reward regular customers. The most common loyalty cards can be found at Boots, Tesco, Sainsbury (Nectar) etc. When the customer buys goods or services they gain points on their card which they can put towards the purchase of more goods and services. Organisations use these cards to gather very valuable information on the spending habits of their customers, allowing them to alter prices and extend special offers.

Market research

This can be either conducted in the **field**, that is, directly with the customers (as detailed above) or at the **desk**, where someone collects information previously collected by someone else (for example, financial reports, government statistics, competitor profiles) and analyses and uses this to the organisation's advantage. Market research considers the product itself, its price, image and place in the market as well as the customer views.

To find out what the customer really experiences, sometimes organisations will employ a **mystery shopper**. This is a person who pretends to shop and experience the service and care ordinary shoppers get. They will record their experiences and evaluate the situation. This information is then fed back to staff either to praise or to reinforce any concerns regarding poor standards. Sometimes staff are aware of the mystery shopper and don't always co-operate and can even be hostile as they feel they are being spied on.

Customer focus groups

Customer focus groups are small groups of customers brought together to provide the organisation with feedback on their goods and services, proposed new products and deletion of lines no longer profitable. The advantage of a focus group is that feedback is immediate, as a predetermined number of people can be invited and controlled. Issues can be clarified and if there is a need to address additional issues it will be easy to do so. Sometimes the focus group is run by a marketing organisation so the participants don't know the company they are reporting on. On other occasions the group will be organised by the company itself so the consumers may not be so objective in their views.

Focus groups can be expensive to run (at the very least, participants' travel expenses need to be paid), and are not held very often, so information from a selected focus group is only a sample of what all customers actually think. In order to get a national perspective, large companies would have to hold focus groups throughout the country – a complicated, expensive and time-consuming exercise which may cause a delay between the organisation's buying of the product and meeting of the group.

Internet Research

Visit the CRM (Customer Relationship Management) website for a very good article on customer focus groups.

Links to this site and other websites relating to Higher Administration can be found at: **www.leckieandleckie.co.uk** by clicking on the Learning Lab button and navigating to the Higher Administration Course Notes page.

o————— **Quick Questions 2** —————o

1 Suggest three ways of improving customer focus in an organisation.

2 Outline the advantages guarantees and warranties offer the customer.

3 List five different methods of market research that can be used to find out customer expectations.

4 Describe the purpose of a store loyalty card.

5 State three reasons why customers do not complain.

Quality management systems

Total quality management (TQM) is a concept that acknowledges that all employees in an organisation have individual as well as collective responsibility for maintaining high quality standards. The fundamental principle of TQM is: *Get it **right**, first time and every time*. The relationship between improving quality and maintaining the business has been demonstrated again and again (especially by the Japanese electronics industry).

Investors in People (IIP) is one of the biggest quality initiatives relating to training and staff development. Organisations wishing to gain IIP status must demonstrate the three key principles which cover 10 areas or indicators grouped by the headings Plan, Do, Review. IIP Status is only awarded to a firm for 3 years, after which they must reapply and prove that they are still meeting the standards.

INVESTORS IN PEOPLE

IIP key principles

● **Plan:** Develop strategies to improve performance of the organisation.

● **Do:** Take action to improve the performance of the organisation.

● **Review:** Evaluate the impact on the performance of the organisation.

Benefits of IIP to the employer	Benefits of IIP to the employee
■ Better morale and a more motivated work force	■ Better recognition and improved job satisfaction
■ Increased productivity and profit	■ Better communication on training and development issues
■ Training needs are more closed linked to business objectives	
■ Increased customer satisfaction	■ Pride in belonging to the organisation
■ Improved reputation for the organisation	■ Supportive working environment
■ Positive publicity	

Quality management allows the setting and monitoring of standards, meeting targets and delivering what has been promised by a courteous and helpful staff. It also allows organisations to measure themselves against other organisations, sometimes known as **benchmarking**. Some of the better known standards are ISO 9000, British Standards BS5750 and the Scottish Quality Management System. For TQM to be successful, quality has to be clearly defined and it must be measurable, and the commitment of all staff is very important.

Communicating with customers

In TQM, communication must be successful with both internal and external customers. Dealing with customers usually happens either face to face or by telephone. Two very important aspects when dealing with the customer are body language and tone of voice. Remember that first impressions count – if an irate customer can be calmed by a pleasant, courteous and competent assistant, then the heat will be taken out of the situation.

Customer service is often undertaken by call centres, and this service is frequently outsourced, sometimes in foreign countries, for example, India. This practice may anger and frustrate some customers if they feel that their complaint is not being recognised as the information is 'too far from home'. The operators are trained to deal with a variety of different queries and enquiries and also in keeping the customer calm. In general this is a relatively cheap and cost-effective method of dealing with customers, and it is an example of when the tone of the voice and the manner in which the customer is treated is very important. (Unfortunately, customers can be confused by the large number of automated call menu options they have to go through before reaching an operator, so they give up before making the complaint.)

Some customers will still put their complaints in writing and this is probably the most effective of methods as it creates a permanent record. Replies to customers can be read and understood and kept for future reference. Email is becoming very popular and can be quicker and more efficient than either a letter or a telephone call. The main drawback of email is that the customer might expect an immediate or at least very prompt response and not all organisations are geared up to do this yet.

With the growth of **e-commerce** many organisations now communicate with their customers by a website. A well designed, easy-to-use and up-to-date website will encourage customers. It will be available 24/7 and as more people gain confidence in using the internet for shopping it will help save costs for the organisation in terms of staff, storage and advertising.

Internet Research

Visit the Biz Ed website to find out more about customer service. Select the Educators link at the right, then select Travel and Tourism. Summarise the key points made in the PowerPoint presentation about customer service, and try the activity on customer service and its benefits.

Links to this site and other websites relating to Higher Administration can be found at: **www.leckieandleckie.co.uk** by clicking on the Learning Lab button and navigating to the Higher Administration Course Notes page.

Extended Response Questions

1 **Compare** the benefits to the organisation and the customer of providing effective customer service. [6 marks]

2 **Identify** and **describe** the key points of a customer complaints policy. [5 marks]

3 **Compare** the use of a mystery shopper with a customer focus group to assess customer opinions. [8 marks]

4 **Justify** why an organisation may become involved with the Investors in People award. [8 marks]

5 **Suggest** how an organisation can test or measure the quality of the service it provides to customers. [6 marks]

6 **Discuss** the importance of different methods of communicating with customers. [4 marks]

6 THE ROLE OF INFORMATION IN DECISION MAKING

What is information?

Staff at all levels of an organisation might be expected to make decisions – and accurate information is essential if reliable decisions are going to be made.

Information is crucial to decision making – but what do we mean by **information**?

Information is the end-product of processed **data**.

Diagrammatically, this could be illustrated in the following way.

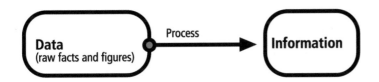

Data: A collection of quantities or facts that have been collected, interpreted and organised in some way. The objective is to process this data in order to give some meaning to it, and the result of the processing will be useful *information*.

Information: Data that has been processed in some way so that it can be used to help decision making and planning activities.

Hint
Make sure you know the difference between *data* and *information*.

Data processing cycle

When we consider the **processing** of data we could be referring to a number of stages. The first stage is the **collection** of the data, and the other stages follow on from this.

The processing stages that data goes through are sometimes referred to as the **data processing cycle**. When data is distributed from one cycle, it may be collected in another.

Examples of how this data may become information include:

- **collecting:** from various sources including email, normal mail, internet
- **checking:** validity of source, currency and sufficiency of data
- **organising:** sort it or group it with other information
- **analysing:** perform summary calculations on it, compare it with standards
- **storing:** file it electronically or in a manual filing system
- **distributing:** send it out via email, internal mail, publish on website or distribute in the normal external mail.

> **Hint**
>
> Memorise the six different stages of the data processing cycle.

Sources of information

Information may come from a variety of sources. Typical sources are:

- paper based, for example, reports, minutes of meetings or trade magazines
- electronic, for example, the internet or CD-ROMs
- oral, for example, presentations, meetings, television.

The source means where something comes from. A piece of information can come from:

- a **primary** *or* a **secondary** source – but not both
- an **internal** *or* an **external** source – but not both.

> **Hint**
>
> You should be aware of the potential strengths and weaknesses (or advantages and disadvantages) of primary and secondary sources and also of internal and external sources so that you can discuss them.

Primary information

Primary information is gathered first-hand by an organisation. It is usually gathered for a specific purpose – perhaps as market research for a new product, or to get feedback from customers on what they think of the company service. It may be gathered through questionnaires, interviews, observation, telephone surveys, etc.

Strengths	Weaknesses
■ It's likely to be up to date. ■ You know its source. ■ It should be correct and relevant for the purpose for which it was gathered.	■ It may be expensive to collect – especially if an external organisation is used, e.g. market research company. ■ It may be difficult to collect. ■ It may be flawed – the sample targeted might be too small, or the questions could be ambiguous or leading. ■ The respondents might have lied. ■ The researcher might be biased and *want* it to show something.

Secondary information

Secondary information is gathered from published sources – you don't need to collect this information, but you need to know where to find it. There are a huge number of possible secondary sources including the internet, newspapers, magazines, books, company reports, timetables and government statistics.

Strengths	Weaknesses
■ There is a wide range of potential sources. ■ Relatively cheap to access.	■ It could be out of date. ■ Your competitors also have access to it. ■ As it hasn't been gathered specifically for you, it might not be relevant to your purpose.

Internal information

Internal information is taken from your own company records. Examples of internal information would be customer records held on a database, company reports or minutes of meetings.

Strengths	Weaknesses
■ It is easy to access. ■ Accurate records will show past performance, making it useful when setting targets and measuring performance. ■ It provides a benchmark for current performance. ■ The analysis of the information will show trends.	■ You need good systems to ensure that information is accurate and up to date. ■ You need staff to set up and manage the information systems – this costs money in training and salaries. ■ New companies may be at a disadvantage as they have little or no information to access.

External information

External information is gathered from outside your organisation. It could be information from other companies (suppliers, competitors, customers), government departments, newspapers, TV or online.

Strengths	Weaknesses
■ It is easy to get hold of. ■ It is relatively cheap to access. ■ It provides information on political, economic, social, technological, environmental and competitive factors (PESTEC).	■ It may be out of date. ■ It takes time to gather it. ■ It is also available to your competitors. ■ It might be biased or unreliable.

Hint

Try to remember at least a couple of strengths and weaknesses for each information source.

Types of information

Information falls into two main types: **quantitative** and **qualitative**.

Quantitative information can be counted or measured. It is usually presented numerically, for example, sales figures, marks obtained in exams or the number of staff in a department. Organisations can use it to help them analyse information, identify trends and make forecasts.

Qualitative information is expressed in words. It involves opinions or judgements. Companies often use it when carrying out customer satisfaction surveys. For example, a survey may ask: 'How do you rate the company's customer service?', and options available may be: excellent, very good, good, acceptable, poor, unacceptable.

Hint

Quantitative and *qualitative* are different – don't get them muddled up!

Quantitative and qualitative information may be presented in a number of ways:

● written, for example, letters, reports, emails, minutes of meetings
● oral, for example, presentations, telephone calls, meetings and conversations
● numerical, for example, numbers and calculations – usually found in tables and spreadsheets
● graphs and pictures, for example, bar graphs, photos and organisation charts.

Each way of presenting information has its advantages and disadvantages.

Written information

Advantages	Disadvantages
■ It can be re-read as often as necessary. ■ It provides a permanent record. ■ It can be stored, whether electronically or in a filing cabinet, so that you can refer back to it.	■ It can take time to produce – so it might be out of date by the time you get it. ■ It may be difficult to get clarification on something.

Oral information

Advantages	Disadvantages
■ It is instant – so should be up to date. ■ It allows for discussion. ■ You can ask questions and get clarification on points. ■ It's a quick way of spreading information.	"But I thought you said..." ■ Different people may interpret it differently. ■ It can easily be forgotten. ■ Difficult to confirm exactly what was said/agreed. ■ If it's important, it should be backed up with a written record.

Numerical information

Advantages	Disadvantages
■ It allows you to make comparisons between sets of data. ■ It is useful for forecasting and projecting trends. ■ Graphs can be produced from it (see below).	■ Many people find figures difficult to understand.

Graphs and pictures

Advantages	Disadvantages
■ Images are often easier to remember than numbers and words. ■ Graphs are good for showing trends. ■ Graphs can be useful when showing comparisons between different sets of data. ■ Organisation charts are used to show the structure of an organisation.	■ Skill is needed to produce an effective chart. ■ Special equipment is needed to produce image. ■ Training staff can be costly.

Quick Questions 1

1 Explain the difference between data and information.
2 Give four stages in the data processing cycle.
3 Outline two internal and two external sources of information.
4 State the difference between quantitative and qualitative information.
5 Suggest two advantages and two disadvantages of written information.

Features of good information

Information has to be good if managers are going to make the right decisions based on it, wherever the information comes from.

You can only make effective decisions if you have high quality information on which to base the decisions. The main characteristics of high quality information are shown below.

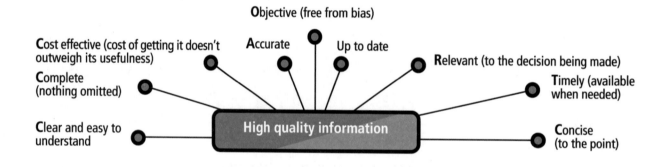

High quality information must be **meaningful** and **useful** to the end user. Knowing who needs the information, and what purpose it will be put to, can help you ensure that it meets these criteria.

Types of decision making

Management is always a decision-making process. Sometimes the decisions are so routine that managers might not even realise that they have made a decision, whereas other decisions will take a lot of analysis, planning and consultation. When making decisions, managers will have to choose a course of action from the alternatives available as they try to meet the objectives that have been set for the business. To manage a business successfully, the right decisions must be made at the right time.

The management in a company falls into three broad categories – **strategic**, **tactical** and **operational**. The types of decision taken at each of these levels vary in several key areas as described opposite and summarised in the table on page 76.

Decision making is making a choice from the different options available.

Strategic decisions

Strategic decisions are made by senior managers and will affect the direction the organisation takes in the long term, perhaps making decisions that will determine the way the company develops over the next 5–10 years. The decisions are concerned with the organisation's strategic objectives – its overall purpose and direction. They often start with 'to improve…', for example, 'to improve efficiency' or 'to improve profitability'. The *scope* of the decisions made is wide and far reaching – they will affect the organisation as a whole, and its overall direction in the future. Most of the information used to help make these decisions will come from external sources, perhaps information on competitors' activities, information from financial institutions on how best to invest profits, or from government departments (home and overseas) on business initiatives and opportunities. The decisions taken are often *high risk* as a wrong decision might ruin the organisation, take a long time to implement, or be very costly to correct.

Tactical decisions

Tactical decisions are made by middle managers and departmental managers and will affect company operations in the medium term. These decisions are about how to achieve the organisation's strategic objectives. For example, if a strategic decision has been taken to improve efficiency, a tactical decision may be to train staff to use more effective working practices. The *scope* of the decisions taken is restricted to those required to ensure the implementation of the strategic plans. The managers will use a mixture of internal and external information to help them make their decisions. They might use information from weekly or monthly reports or sales analysis data sheets to help them monitor activities and check that targets are being met, and make decisions on how to rectify things if they are not. Or they could use information on competitors' activities as a benchmark to measure their own performance. The decisions are usually considered to be *medium risk* as any bad decisions may take time and money to fix, but should not jeopardise the overall success of the organisation.

Operational decisions

Operational decisions are the day-to-day decisions that need to be made. Staff at all levels can make operational decisions, but most are made by section managers and shift managers. The *scope* is limited to the immediate resolution of problems as they arise, and most of the information required will come from internal sources. They are considered *low risk* as a wrong decision may result in things being difficult for a while, but it should be relatively easy to fix.

Quick Questions 2

1. What level of management would make the following decisions:
   a to open a new factory in Calcutta
   b deciding how best to market a new product
   c the day and time for the weekly team meeting
   d whether or not to market the company products on the internet
   e whether to offer voluntary redundancy to staff
   f the training requirements and allocation of training budget within a department
   g to buy out a competitor.
2. State six features of good information.
3. Explain the term 'scope' with regard to decision making.
4. Suggest who would make the decisions at strategic, tactical and operational levels.
5. Give a disadvantage of working with numerical information.

Types of decision taken at strategic, tactical and operational levels			
	TYPE OF DECISION		
	Strategic	**Tactical**	**Operational**
Time span	Long-term – decisions will affect the organisation for a number of years	Medium-term – typically affecting the operation of the business over a period of 6–12 months	Short-term – affecting the operation of the business over a period of anything from a few hours to a few months
Scope	Set the aims and objectives of the organisation	Implementation of strategic decisions	Day-to-day decisions to ensure that targets are met and standards achieved
Main source of information	External	Internal/External	Internal
Risk level	High risk	Medium risk	Low risk
Decision makers	Top level management, e.g. board of directors, chief executive, heads of departments	Middle level management, e.g. senior staff, factory manager	Lower level managers, e.g. supervisors, team leaders
Examples	■ Taking over a rival company ■ Expanding marketing activities overseas ■ Opening a new factory or branch ■ Increasing the company product range ■ Changing the organisation's structure	■ Adjusting staffing levels in a department ■ Changing office layout to open plan ■ Introducing new working arrangements to a factory ■ Deciding on overall stock levels to be held	■ Scheduling of leave arrangements ■ Allocation of duties to staff to ensure that weekly production targets are met ■ Deciding on meeting schedule for department

---

⚬————————— Extended Response Questions —————⚬

1 **Explain** what these terms mean in relation to quality of information:

concise   timely   relevant   [6 marks]

2 **Identify** the three levels of management and **describe** one example of the type of decision that each level may take.   [6 marks]

3 **Compare** qualitative and quantitative information.   [6 marks]

4 **Justify** two of the stages in the data processing cycle.   [8 marks]

5 **Discuss** the strengths and weaknesses of primary and secondary information.   [8 marks]

7 THE IMPACT OF ICT ON WORK PRACTICES AND MANAGEMENT OF INFORMATION

Impact of ICT on workflow

Information and communication technology (ICT) has had a huge impact on the way that work flows through an organisation.

When considering workflow, regardless of whether or not ICT is used, the stages are:

The impact of ICT can be seen clearly in each of these areas.

The most noticeable effect that ICT has had on workflow is:

- **speed** – information can be located, produced, updated and transmitted much more quickly
- **ease of access** – it is relatively easy to find information within and outwith the organisation.

Activities and features that have had a particular effect on workflow at each stage are described below.

Input

- Information can be **keyed in once** and then used by many people.
- The fact that data doesn't need to be keyed in several times should result in the data being more **accurate** (although it is essential that the data is keyed in accurately in the first place).
- Data held in different formats can be input – keyed in, copied in, scanned in or read in by optical character recognition or optical mark recognition systems.
- Input can be restricted through the use of logins and passwords – this can help ensure data integrity and contributes to greater accuracy.
- The use of drop-down lists, check boxes, radio buttons and validation checks can help reduce the number of errors made during data input.
- Information can be gathered from a wide geographical area, for example, using email, electronic databases and the internet.
- Search and retrieval processes ensure that you can get the data you require from both inside and outside the organisation – often very quickly.

Processing

- The same data can be processed in many ways to produce different outputs, for example, customer data could be processed to give lists, labels or merged letters, while statistics in a spreadsheet could be displayed in a data sheet, as a graph or copied into a report produced using a word processor.
- Processing data by computer results in documents being produced accurately and quickly, for example, it is possible to extract data that meets specific criteria from a huge database in seconds – a job that could take days or weeks if we didn't use ICT.

- Data can be held centrally, so that all staff can access and process it to suit their purposes. This helps ensure that all staff are using the same version of the data held and makes it easier to keep it up to date.
- Provided the shared data is accurate and up to date it will facilitate better decision making at all levels of the organisation.
- Fewer people are required to perform routine tasks such as copying and distributing mail because organisations usually use email for these activities. This can result in reduced staff costs as fewer people may be needed to do the work.
- Files can be accessed by several members of staff at the same time – this results in less time being wasted as staff do not have to wait for another member of staff to finish with a file before they can use it.

Output

- Standard layout and templates ensures a corporate look for company documents which helps contribute to a professional image.
- Standard layout means that staff and customers get used to where they can find the information they require, so it takes them less time to make sense of a document.
- Text, numbers, graphics, sound and video can all be integrated into the output.
- The resulting output can be formatted to look very professional.
- Output can be distributed at any time of the day and recipients can access information sent to them when it suits them – this can be particularly useful when working across time zones.
- Information can be distributed by email or via the internet, for example, posted on a website, which means people all over the world can get the information very quickly.
- The output can be sent to different media, for example, paper, website, personal digital assistant (PDA), email.
- Supervisors can easily access any output if they wish to check it before distribution.
- Information can be transmitted very quickly – by email if it is already in an electronic format or it can be faxed if it isn't.

Hint

You should be able to discuss how ICT has made a difference to workflow, that is, it has made the input and processing of data and output of information faster. It has also made it much easier and quicker to locate the information that you require, especially if it is held electronically.

Quick Questions 1

1 Identify one effect that ICT has had on workflow at the input, processing and output stages.
2 Give two examples, when considering workflow, of how the use of ICT may reduce the use of paper.

Main features of software applications and networks

You should be able to discuss the main features, and the advantages and the disadvantages of the most commonly used business software applications that you have used throughout this course. You should also be able to discuss networks – in particular local area networks (LANs) and wide area networks (WANs). Although we would normally consider the benefits of using networks to outweigh any disadvantages that they may have, you should be able to identify and discuss any disadvantages too.

Application	Overview	Main features	Advantages
Word processing	Text processing system used to produce letters, reports, minutes, forms (paper-based and electronic), etc.	■ Tables ■ Mail merge ■ Standard text ■ Columns ■ Page layouts ■ Electronic forms ■ Integration with spreadsheet, database, presentation software	■ Improved speed and accuracy as a result of using standard layout and text ■ Amendments can be made quickly and easily ■ Automation of some routines, e.g. mail merge ■ Wide range of alternative layouts can be achieved relatively easily ■ Data collection via electronic forms can be used to populate a database table
Spreadsheet	Used to perform calculations, analyse and present numeric data effectively	■ Performs calculations using a variety of operators, e.g. +, -. *, / and % ■ Automates calculations by using functions, e.g. sum, minimum ■ Sophisticated formatting and charting capabilities	■ Routine calculations can virtually be automated, e.g. weekly/monthly salary calculations ■ Data can be stored and reused ■ Data and calculations can be easily updated ■ Data can be analysed in different ways, e.g. IF functions, CountIF, >, < ■ Data can be produced graphically which can aid interpretation
Database	Stores vast amounts of data, e.g. on staff, customers, students	■ Data can be sorted quickly ■ Subsets of data can be extracted quickly ■ Information held in tables and queries can be displayed effectively using reports	■ Data can be stored in one place and accessed by staff throughout the organisation provided they have access rights ■ Easier to keep data up to date ■ Provided data is up to date and accurate, better quality decisions can be made by everyone
Presentation	Used to produce slides and supporting documents, e.g. handouts	■ Integration of text, numbers, tables, charts, organisation charts, etc. on slides ■ Animation effects add interest to slides	■ A good presentation can significantly enhance the audience's understanding of the information being presented ■ Corporate image can be presented by use of standard templates ■ Variety of objects can be used, e.g. graphics, which can aid understanding

Application	Overview	Main features	Advantages
Email	A fast, efficient and cost-effective way to send messages anywhere in the world	■ Electronic means of sending text and data ■ Files (including graphics and audio) can be attached to a message ■ The same message can be sent to many people at the same time	■ It is fast and relatively cheap ■ Recipients can view their mail at a time that suits them ■ Good when working across time zones ■ You can send electronic files to people, e.g. reports and spreadsheets ■ Can usually be accessed anywhere with an internet connection
E-diary	Electronic calendar and personal organiser	■ Calendar for noting appointments and meetings ■ Task list for keeping track of all the things you have to do ■ Notes feature for quick reminders	■ Easy to enter/amend/move/delete appointments, tasks and notes ■ Everything is in one place which makes it easier to keep track of your schedule and check what you should be doing
Local Area Network (LAN)	Connects computers and peripherals within a local area, e.g. a building	■ Consists of workstations (usually PCs or Macs), peripherals (printers, scanners), and servers (central computers where data is stored or that control printing and email). These devices are usually connected by cables or in some cases are wireless	■ Easy for many workstations to share peripherals, e.g. printers (cheaper than everyone having their own printer) ■ Access to central storage area makes it easier to share files and databases ■ Provided all files are stored on servers, back-ups can be taken of all data – making it less likely that data gets lost
Wide Area Network (WAN)	A network that connects computers on a global scale	■ Connects computer systems over wide geographical areas ■ Allows for fast transmission of data over long distances ■ Most people associate WANs with the internet – a global network of computers – but a WAN can be used to connect different branches of an organisation anywhere in the world	■ Speed at which data can be transmitted between branches of an organisation ■ Facility to send email anywhere in the world via WANs ■ Gives easy access to the internet and the world wide web ■ Facility to have a 'secure' link to sites that transmit sensitive data, e.g. company data or financial transactions

> ### Hint
> Make sure you know the main features and potential benefits of the business software you have used.

Disadvantages of using business software

The advantages of using business software far outweigh any disadvantages – but if you are asked to suggest any disadvantages you could mention: the cost of purchasing the software, the time and expense of training staff to use the software, and the effort taken to implement procedures to ensure confidentiality and security of the information. (See pages 88–90 for more information on organisational procedures for security and confidentiality of information.)

Networks

Local area networks

There are basically two types of LAN – peer-to-peer and client–server.

Peer-to-peer networks are sometimes used by small organisations that only have a few computers, for example, between two and five. The computers are linked together using cables, and can share peripherals such as printers and scanners and also have access to each others' hard drives. They are cheap, and don't really need much technical expertise to link them together. They are only really suitable for small networks (imagine what it would be like if you had 20 or more linked together – any time you tried to save or open a file you would have 20 or more drives to choose from!).

Client–server networks are used by most organisations. In this network there are a number of powerful central computers (the **servers**) that are used for file storage, print management and managing network traffic, including email. Each user has their own PC (called a **client**) linked to the server(s).

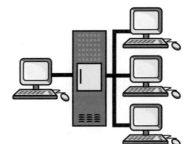

The advantages of LAN are given in the table opposite. Potential **disadvantages** include:

- the cost of installing and supporting the network
- if the network goes down, no-one can access files needed for their work
- if the file server is damaged or stolen, all data may be lost (which is why it is important to have back-ups)
- a **virus** can spread very quickly across a LAN once it is in
- it could be easy for an unhappy employee to damage or corrupt company data.

Wide area networks

Again, the advantages of WAN are given in the table opposite. Potential **disadvantages** include:

- people outside the organisation have a route in to your company data – it is therefore very important to have appropriate access controls and security procedures in place to limit the areas that are accessible
- you have no control over external websites that you use. Web pages can be removed from the internet, or the content changed by the owner, so pages that were once useful to you may no longer be available or useful.

Hint

When considering networks, you should also be able to identify and discuss any potential *disadvantages* that may be associated with them as well as the *advantages*.

E-commerce

As our business use of networks and in particular the internet has increased, e-commerce has become an important asset to many organisations.

E-commerce (also called **e-business**) is the buying and selling of goods and services electronically, usually over the internet.

Some organisations do *all* their business electronically, for example, Amazon and eBay. Other organisations use e-commerce as *one* way of reaching their potential customer base.

Advantages of e-commerce to the organisation include:

● customer base – you have a global customer base for your products
● premises – you have the opportunity to grow your business without expanding your premises, or without opening an office or outlet in an expensive area
● opening hours – 24/7 (unless the system goes down), with no overtime to pay!
● overheads – increased business potential without increasing your staffing and running costs (although you will need to pay to keep your website up to date)
● marketing costs – potentially reduced as you should have your site registered with the major search engines and then customers should be able to find your site when searching for the type of products or services that you sell (although you would probably still advertise in local papers, trade magazines, radio, etc.).

Potential **disadvantages** to the organisation include:

● the time and cost of getting a good website set up
● ensuring you have very secure systems in place so that customers know they are safe when conducting business electronically with you – no-one wants to give their personal details or exchange money electronically if they do not think it is safe to do so. However, the advantages mean that an increasing number of organisations are set up for e-commerce.

Advantages of e-commerce to the customer include:

● they can browse and buy 24/7
● they have easy access to suppliers worldwide
● they can compare products and prices at their leisure
● there are no pushy sales people to deal with
● there is no need to travel to the company to buy
● products are delivered to the customer.

Potential **disadvantages** to the customer include:

● they cannot actually see the product 'in the flesh' – although they could check it out at a local store and then buy online if the price is better
● the organisation or supplier becomes faceless – some companies are much better than others at dealing with any problems
● a badly designed website can make it difficult to find the required information, which can be frustrating and potentially offputting if the customer feels they are wasting a lot of time and still not finding what they want.

"Yes, but how does it *feel*?"

Hint

You should be able to discuss the pros and cons of e-commerce for the *customer* as well as the *organisation*.

Quick Questions 2

1 List three features that could be used on a form created using word processing software.
2 Suggest three potential benefits of using database software to store customer records.
3 Give two examples of electronic communication methods.
4 State one advantage and one disadvantage that could be associated with a LAN.
5 Identify two benefits e-commerce will give an organisation.

The impact of ICT on work practices

The use of ICT has had a considerable effect on our working practices. The main areas are summarised in the diagram below.

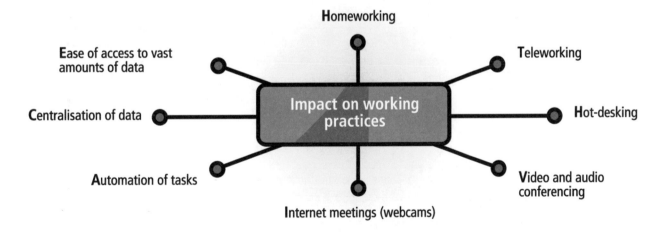

As with all such changes there are advantages and disadvantages to be considered.

Hint

See Chapter 2 for additional information on the effect of ICT on work practices.

Change	Advantages	Disadvantages
Use of ICT allows more flexible working practices, e.g. homeworking, teleworking	■ Allows for a better work–life balance for many people ■ No need to travel to the office each day – saves time and money, and is more environmentally friendly ■ Organisations can perhaps function from smaller premises as staff can work almost anywhere they choose ■ Easy to distribute information to people at any location – at home or when they are on the move	■ Sometimes difficult to separate your work life and personal life if it all happens under the one roof ■ Staff may feel isolated and miss the social buzz of working in an office ■ Staff may find it difficult to discipline and motivate themselves to get their work done if there are other distractions, e.g. domestic tasks ■ Difficult to control health and safety aspects when staff work at home ■ Can lead to disagreements between staff and the organisation on who is responsible for practical aspects, e.g. paying for equipment, insurance policies, electricity and broadband, and what is an acceptable work/personal balance in the use of the equipment
Hot-desking	■ Company does not need to have a desk for each employee – which reduces space needed and cost of premises	■ Staff often like their own space to work in and feel uncomfortable in a depersonalised environment ■ Staff have to clear their desks of everything when they finish work so that someone else can use the desk
Routine tasks can be performed using fewer staff	■ Tasks are often performed quicker when using ICT ■ Companies can save money previously spent on staff in some areas ■ Machines make fewer errors than humans when performing routine tasks, e.g. sorting a list of data	■ Humans usually put the data into the system and tell it what to do – any errors they make can quickly become big errors, e.g. wrong bills sent out to customers. Remember: garbage in, garbage out!
Centralisation of company data into vast databases	■ All staff have access to the same data ■ Easier to keep the data up to date and accurate ■ Appropriate back-up procedures can be organised ■ Helps company deliver a better service to customers	■ If data is inaccurate or not up to date, wrong decisions will be made throughout the organisation ■ If central server goes down, no-one can get the data that they need to do their work
Internet meetings/ webcams/video and audio conferencing	■ Facilitate meetings globally, without people having to spend time and money travelling ■ You can see and hear each other so it is relatively easy to clarify any points that need to be addressed ■ You can exchange files electronically during the meeting, or show things on everyone's screen when discussing issues	■ Not everyone is comfortable with this type of meeting ■ There are usually very strict time restrictions (especially if a facility has been specially booked), so things can get rushed ■ If the technology lets you down, the meeting has to be abandoned

1 Give two examples of the potential problems of homeworking.

2 Define the term 'hot-desking'.

3 List three developments that have contributed to the adoption of more flexible working patterns.

Data management systems

Many companies often give huge numbers of people (both internal and external to the organisation) access to different sets of the data and information that they hold, so it is essential that this data and information is **organised** and **protected**. In other words, the **data** must be **managed**.

Data management is all about setting up systems, procedures and controls relating to the way in which data is: input, stored and retrieved.

Data management is also concerned with establishing and managing procedures that control:

- who has access to the data and information
- how it is kept up to date
- how it is kept secure.

The whole point of good data management is to maximise the benefits that the information gives to the organisation. This in turn should help to increase the effectiveness of the organisation.

To help ensure good data management across an organisation, many organisations will have a **centralised** computer section – often called something like *Information Systems, Information Services, Computer Services* or *Management Information Services*. This department will have responsibility for some, if not all, of the following activities:

- purchase of hardware and software
- maintenance of hardware and software
- setting up systems and procedures
- user policies
- codes of practice
- ICT training
- support systems, for example, IT help desk
- production of user guides for staff.

Although some organisations allow individual departments to operate their own systems, this is not usually the most effective way of doing things. It can result in incompatibility problems because different software or versions of software are used by different departments. It can also make training and the production of user guides more difficult and expensive if everyone is not using the same systems. Different departments may also have different standards, codes of practice and procedures. So it is usually much better to centralise this service and develop a professional team that look after this area for the organisation as a whole.

The **advantages** of a centralised IT department are:

- the department has an overview of organisational data requirements and performance
- it is easier to standardise the computer hardware and software used (giving fewer compatibility problems across the organisation)
- standardised systems and procedures can be put in place – so everyone is working to the same rules
- it is easier to prioritise the purchase of new hardware and software across the company, and budget accordingly
- it is easier to control what hardware and software are used, and have procedures on how they should be used
- the department can build up its expertise and specialisation and keep abreast of new developments so it can advise users on the best IT solution for them
- it is easier and cheaper to train and support users if they are all working with similar systems.

non-centralised IT service centralised IT service

A potential **disadvantage** of centralisation is that 'one hat doesn't necessarily fit all' – some sections of the organisation may feel that they have particular needs that are not properly addressed by a centralised functional area.

Whether or not this function is centralised, it is essential that appropriate hardware and software are used to optimise the performance of the data management system. Areas to consider in relation to hardware include:

- **Selection of appropriate hardware** is important as this can affect the speed of the system – the speed of storage and retrieval of data, printing, email, internet access, etc.
- **Keeping up to date** with developments is essential if an organisation is to take advantage of the latest technological advances. Having specialists makes it easier to keep abreast of developments in this fast-changing environment. This is usually a better option than having to rely on the enthusiastic amateur who has to try and do it along with their 'real' job.
- **Processor speed, hard-drive and memory capacity** affect the speed and capability of a system. A rolling update programme for hardware will help ensure optimum effectiveness of data systems.
- **Storage and retrieval devices** also affect the capability of your system; these include hard-drives, DVDs, CD-ROMs, CD-RW, pen-drives and zip disks. The most appropriate storage device will depend on the volume of data involved, how often it is updated, and how often it needs to be backed up, etc.
- **Input devices** – keyboards and mice are the most widely used, but touch screens, hand-held devices, scanners, optical character recognition (OCR), and voice recognition systems all have their place. However, light pens, magnetic ink character recognition (MICR), smart cards, barcode readers and optical mark recognition systems are more appropriate in some environments.

Areas to consider in relation to software include:

- **Operating system software** – this is used to set up folder structures for your data, provide an interface between your hardware and application software and control the operation of the computer system as a whole.
- **Utility programmes** – these include virus checkers, defragmenting utilities, software to check user IDs and passwords, etc. and many of them are very important when considering the security of your data.

Electronic file management

Electronic file management is part of the data management process. File management is all about the organisation and manipulation of your computer files.

Different organisations will have their own file management procedures, and you should become familiar with the procedures used by any organisation you work for.

Electronic file management procedures should provide guidance on:

- file location
- folder structures and file names

- version control
- housekeeping procedures
- back-up procedures.

File location

There should be information on *where* files should be stored, for example, which drive(s) contain forms and templates, or which drive you should store your personal work files on. Storing your data in the correct place is important as it might affect if, or how often, it is backed up.

Folder structures and file names

Guidelines on folder structures, folder names and file names should be given. If people adhere to these it will make it easier for other staff to find the files if they need to share them, or if staff move jobs or are off work.

Version control

If you keep different versions of the same file, version control procedures should be followed. This will help ensure that you and others know which version of a file you have and whether or not it is the most up-to-date version. For example:

- the first draft of a report may be given the name *Project Report – 010207* (to show that the report was created on 1 February 2007)
- an amended version of this report may then be saved and called *Project Report – 210207*
- the final version of the report may be called *Project Report – 010307 – Final*.

Everyone needs to know how to name each version, so it is obvious which reports are the draft versions and which one is definitely the final one.

Housekeeping procedures

There should be guidelines on when to delete files or where to archive old files to. This will help ensure that the servers do not end up full of old files, which can result in the system performance being compromised.

Back-up procedures

Back-up procedures should be outlined, with details of who is responsible for it, and how often it is done.

> **Hint**
>
> You need to know the difference between *data management* and *file management*. Data management ensures that data is organised and protected. File management is part of the data management process and gives guidance on where files should be stored, how folders and files should be named, version control procedures, etc.

Consequences of poor data management

Data management and file management are extremely important when everyone is using the same databases and files for their work. It is vitally important that an organisation has procedures for data and file management and that staff are trained in the procedures and adhere to them.

If procedures are in place, and followed, then there should be few problems. However, if there are no procedures, or they are not followed, then the consequences will include:

- staff (including yourself) having difficulty in finding files
- time wasted in trying to locate files
- frustration and annoyance for staff
- business activities being slowed down as a result of time wasted
- general confusion as no-one knows where files are or what they are called
- systems slowing down as disks and servers fill up with files
- errors being made if the wrong version of a file is used
- potentially costly decisions made by management if they are working with out-of-date information
- breakdown in customer relations as they lose patience if errors are made, for example, addresses are lost, orders are not met, information is not sent out
- legal implications if data is not held securely or is mishandled.

Poor data management can cost an organisation money – because of time that is wasted, errors made, customers lost and staff demotivated.

Hint

You should be able to discuss the implications of poor data management.

Quick Questions 4

1 Define the term 'data management'.
2 Suggest why good data management is important.
3 List three activities that a centralised computer services department would be responsible for.
4 Identify three areas in which the hardware selected may influence the effectiveness of a data management system.
5 List three areas that file management procedures should address.
6 Identify three potential consequences of poor file management.

Organisational procedures for security and confidentiality of information

Ensuring the **security** and **integrity** of company data has become a major issue for all companies. Consideration must also be given to the **privacy** and **confidentiality** of data.

Security means protecting data against: theft, damage and destruction.

Integrity means ensuring that the data is: accurate, up to date and error free.

Privacy means that the data must be held securely so that only those who need access to the data can access it.

Confidentiality means that those who do have access to the data respect it, and do not discuss it with others that do not have a right to know what it says.

Organisations have a responsibility to:

- undertake a **risk analysis** – to identify and quantify the risks that their data is exposed to
- put **countermeasures** in place – procedures and systems that reduce or remove the identified risks.

Organisations need to consider:

- physical security of hardware and software
- back-up procedures
- access rights.

Physical threats include theft, damage to equipment by people (intentional or accidental) and damage from disasters, such as fire and flood.

Minimising damage from physical threats

- Ensure offices are locked and windows are closed when buildings are empty.
- Alarm the buildings so that warning is given of intrusions.
- Use cameras and surveillance equipment to monitor the premises at all times.
- Restrict the number of access points to the building.
- Keep visitors away from computer areas.
- Have security guards/dogs patrol the grounds at night.
- Keep lights on in the grounds at night.
- Train staff on how to move equipment.
- Provide trolleys for transporting items (to minimise the chances of equipment being dropped).
- Keep fire doors closed to limit the spread of any fires.
- Have fire fighting equipment and train staff how to use it.
- Install sprinkler systems to help put fires out.
- Lag pipes to reduce the chance of them bursting in winter.
- Take out adequate insurance – so that if the worst does happen, you can recover from it.

Threats to the software and data include:

- theft – if servers, hard drives or laptops are stolen, then the data on them goes too
- disk damage and corruption, making files unusable. This may be as a result of component failure or a virus
- physical damage resulting in corrupted files, perhaps as a result of malicious or accidental damage, fire or theft, etc.

Minimising disruption caused by problems

- Store the original software CDs and DVDs securely, for example, in a safe or locked cabinet, away from the servers and PCs – the software can then be re-installed on another system if necessary.
- Back-up all data files regularly – you can then copy the back-ups on to new drives if necessary.
- The company should have an insurance policy, to help it replace equipment and software.
- Key staff should be aware of the disaster recovery plan, so that if the worst does happen, someone knows what to do to get things up and running again.

Access rights

Access rights means controlling or restricting access to those people who are authorised to use the data.

It is important that anyone who needs access to the data to do their job has it – but it is equally important that those that do not need access to the data cannot see it. It is often the case that users get access to some of the data in the databases, for example, an HR assistant may have access to contact and qualification data relating to staff, but may not be authorised to see confidential information such as salary, bank details, or details of disciplinary procedures.

Access rights can be set at different levels, for example, read only, read write, no access. Security procedures to restrict access include:

- **log in procedures:** to ensure that only those with a legitimate login get access
- **password:** to double-check the identity of the person logging in.

Paper-based files

Organisations are also responsible for ensuring the security and confidentiality of data held in paper-based systems.

When considering paper-based files, procedures should be in place to ensure that:

- files are returned to the filing cabinet after use
- filing cabinets are locked and keys are stored somewhere safe, for example, locked in a desk drawer
- papers are not left at the photocopier
- all papers are collected from printers promptly
- papers are not left lying on desks unattended
- papers are shredded or disposed of properly.

Hint

Although this unit is primarily concerned with the management of electronic data you should also give consideration to the management of paper-based files.

Quick Questions 5

1 Differentiate between data security and data integrity.
2 What is meant by the 'confidentiality' of data?
3 Identify two possible threats to computer hardware and suggest a way of reducing the risk posed by each threat.
4 List two possible consequences of having a poor back-up procedure.
5 Suggest two ways of ensuring the security of information that is paper based.

You should be able to discuss, and know the implications of, the main Acts that affect the use of ICT and the data stored on computerised systems.

Data Protection Act 1984 and 1998

The main purpose of this Act is to balance the rights of those that lawfully hold our data for processing purposes, and our own rights.

Key words that you must understand when discussing the Data Protection Act are:

- **personal data** – data about a living individual
- **data subject** – the individual that the data is about (you and me). We have rights that must not be infringed by organisations that hold and process our data
- **data controller** – the individual or organisation that holds the data; this could be your school, college, bank, employer, library, hospital, a company that you have bought something from, etc. Data controllers have certain obligations that they must adhere to when holding and processing personal data.

Data controller obligations	Rights of individual
They must notify the Information Commissioner's Office to let them know what personal data they are holding, and why. They must also pay a fee and register as a data controller.	The rights of the individual are clearly defined by the Data Protection Act and include:
There are **eight** data protection principles that a data controller must adhere to. Data must be:	■ **subject access:** you can find out what is held on computer about you
1 fairly and lawfully obtained and processed (see below)	■ **prevent processing:** you can ask a data controller not to process your information
2 accurate and up to date	■ **direct marketing:** you can ask that your data is not used for direct marketing
3 adequate, relevant and not excessive	■ **automatic decision making:** you can object to decisions being made on your behalf on account of the data held
4 processed for limited purposes	
5 held securely	■ **compensation:** you can claim compensation for damage or distress if the Act is breached
6 not retained for longer than necessary	
7 processed in accordance with the individual's rights	■ **rectify, block, erase and destroy:** if the data is not accurate or has opinions based on inaccurate information you can apply to the courts to force the data controller to rectify, block, erase or destroy the data.
8 not be transferred to countries outside the EU unless the country has adequate protection for the individual.	

For data to be considered *fairly* processed it must fall into at least one of the following categories:

- the data subject must have consented to the processing
- the processing must be necessary
- the processing is necessary under a legal obligation, for example, disclosure to check for criminal records of anyone working with minors
- the processing is necessary to protect the interests of the data subject
- it is needed to carry out a public function, for example, in court
- it is necessary to pursue the legitimate interests of the data controller or third parties (unless it could unjustifiably prejudice the interest of the individual).

Sensitive personal information

This includes information on ethnic origin, political opinions, religion, trade union membership, physical and mental health, sexual orientation, criminal proceedings or convictions. Any organisation intending to record and process this type of information must meet at least one of the following conditions:

- they have the explicit consent of the individual (the data subject)
- the information is required by law for employment purposes (for example, criminal record when working with children)
- the processing of the information is necessary to protect the vital interests of the individual or another person
- they are dealing with the judicial process or law administration.

The role of the Information Commissioner

You can ask the Commissioner to assess whether the Acts have been contravened.

Internet Research

Visit the Privacy Data Protection website to find information about the DPA or recent cases. Summarise any breaches made by organisations and how they intend to rectify them.

An interesting report on problems with SQA exam results in 2000 and how these related to DPA is given on the Silicon website.

Links to these sites and other websites relating to Higher Administration can be found at: **www.leckieandleckie.co.uk** by clicking on the Learning Lab button and navigating to the Higher Administration Course Notes page.

Freedom of Information Act 2000

The Data Protection Acts have been amended by the introduction of the Freedom of Information (FOI) Act. The FOI Act:

- applies to public authorities
- gives a statutory right to information
- provides for the release of exempt information in the public interest.

To comply with FOI legislation, public authorities must:

- establish a publication scheme which means they commit to publishing information
- classify what information they will publish, such as staff policies. This could be expanded to explain what this means, for example, procedures that staff should follow and information on the behaviour expected from staff when they are at work
- indicate if there will be a charge for publishing the information.

The FOI Act means that information previously regarded as 'secret' will ultimately be available to everyone.

Copyright, Designs and Patents Act 1988

Copyright gives the authors of written and recorded works rights about how their works can be used. The works covered by the Act include books, film, music and computer programs. The purpose of the Act is to ensure that exclusive ownership of the work is retained, and no unauthorised copying of the work takes place.

The Act gives the author or owner rights over their material regarding:

- copying, adapting and distributing
- electronic communication (including broadcasting)
- renting or lending to the public
- public performance of the work.

The Act covers materials as soon as they are published or recorded, whether in books, film, music or computer programs.

If you would like to use someone's work, you may be able to get permission to do so from the author, but there is usually a fee involved.

Some organisations, for example, education authorities or colleges, pay a **blanket fee** to a specialist agency that collects the fees and distributes any money collected to the authors, composers or performers (usually on an annual basis). This fee allows them to copy extracts from the materials concerned without having to ask permission every time they want to copy something. The agency for printed works is called the Copyright Licensing Agency, and there are similar agencies for video performance and performing rights.

In an office environment or when studying, it is most likely that you will want to copy written material. If your organisation pays a blanket fee (see above) there will be a poster beside the photocopier telling you what and how much you are allowed to photocopy.

In addition to this, you are also permitted to photocopy printed materials if you are:

- copying them for your private study
- copying them to review them
- using them for non-profit making research
- reporting on current events
- using them for judicial purposes
- copying them for educational use.

If you take multiple copies of something, or copy a large part of a work, you may still need to obtain the copyright holder's permission.

If you are using the material to help you prepare a paper, you should acknowledge your source by giving the author and title of the publication in your final script. Copyright indicators include:

© **Caroline Patterson and Moira Stephen**

or

All rights reserved

or

No part of this publication may be reproduced or transmitted in any form or by any means without permission.

Organisations also have to be careful not to infringe copyright when it comes to using computer software. Each organisation must ensure that:

- they have purchased enough licences for their use
- employees do not copy software
- the content of CD-ROMs is not printed and copied
- CDs and software are not copied
- information from the internet is not copied without permission.

Websites can be accessed from anywhere in the world, so the owner of a website may find it difficult to enforce UK copyright laws on those who access the site from outside the UK.

> ## Hint
> Don't make the mistake of thinking that material that you find on the internet is copyright free. You may still need to get approval to use it.

The Computer Misuse Act 1990

This Act makes it illegal to carry out offences against computer systems or the data held on the systems. There are three specific offences identified within the Computer Misuse Act, and these relate to:

- unauthorised access to computer material
- unauthorised access with the intention of committing further offences
- unauthorised modification of computer material.

It is an offence to access computer material that you have not been authorised to access, for example, it is an offence to log on to a computer system using the login details of a colleague or friend. This offence applies to people that hack into computer systems too – even if they do no damage.

It is also an offence to access a computer system with the intention of committing other offences, for example, deleting or modifying data. You commit an offence even if you do not succeed in your ultimate aim.

Finally, it is an offence to delete or modify information on a computer system if you have not been authorised to do so. Many organisations limit the number of people who are allowed to update the data on their system, giving limited 'read only' access to most people who need access.

Internet Research

Visit the BBC GCSE Bitesize website and find information about the main features of the different Acts relating to privacy and security of information.

Links to this site and other websites relating to Higher Administration can be found at: **www.leckieandleckie.co.uk** by clicking on the Learning Lab button and navigating to the Higher Administration Course Notes page.

Quick Questions 6

1 List three principles of the Data Protection Act.
2 Give one right that the data subject has under the Data Protection Act.
3 If your organisation pays a blanket fee to allow limited photocopying of certain printed materials, where would you usually expect to find information on what and how much you are allowed to copy?
4 Give one example of how an organisation might infringe copyright law when using software.
5 Give one offence identified in the Computer Misuse Act.

Extended Response Questions

1 **Discuss** the impact of ICT on workflow within an organisation. [6 marks]

2 **Describe** the benefits of using reports to present data extracted from a database system. [6 marks]

3 **Justify** the decision to implement an e-business solution to advertise and sell your company's products. [6 marks]

4 **Identify** four security risks that could affect ICT resources, and **suggest** preventative steps that an organisation could take to protect itself from those risks. [8 marks]

5 **Discuss** the potential **consequences** of poor electronic file management procedures. [6 marks]

6 **Identify** two pieces of legislation that staff using ICT should be familiar with, and **suggest** working practices that they should adopt to prevent them falling foul of the law. [8 marks]

The tasks in this chapter will help you prepare for Paper 2. Paper 2 assesses your practical ICT skills, and you will be asked to complete a set of tasks within a 1 hour 20 minute period. The tasks will assess your database, spreadsheet and word processing skills. Paper 2 is worth 60 marks.

No instructions are provided on how to perform the tasks in this chapter – it is assumed that you know how to use the software, and are ready for some exam preparation. You can access the 'Help' facility on the computer but remember this will lose you time in the exam.

The **files** that you require for the tasks in this chapter can be found on the Leckie and Leckie website. Go to: **www.leckieandleckie.co.uk** and then click on the Learning Lab button. Navigate to the Higher Administration Course Notes page. Download the files for this section and save them on to your own computer before you start.

A summary of the **new skills** that you should have built up at Higher level is displayed on the following pages. The exam will contain a sample of the areas identified. There is no way of knowing exactly what will be sampled, so make sure you can perform the various tasks in your applications.

In total, there are **three sets of practice tasks** for you to work through. There are some general tips before the first set of tasks and it would be useful to read these before attempting each set of tasks.

For the first set of tasks, **suggested answers** are printed in this book, showing how possible marks may be awarded (suggested answers to the second and third sets are given on the Leckie and Leckie website). There are some tasks that can be completed satisfactorily in more than one way, and alternative acceptable responses are suggested where appropriate. There are also hints on how you could have tackled a task in the suggested **marking guidelines**.

However you solve a problem, or present your solution, your work should be **accurate**, **well presented** and follow an acceptable **house style**.

Hint

You may wish to **time** yourself and complete each set under **closed book exam conditions.** Alternatively you might prefer to work through the exercises using the solutions as a guide. Remember that these tasks also test your problem-solving skills and you will be expected to know which software to choose to solve the business problem and be able to use your initiative to produce a result that is fit for purpose.

The following table summarises the features and functions you should be familiar with at **Higher** level. It is assumed that you are fully conversant with *all* requirements at **Intermediate 2** level, as any of the ICT skills developed at that level may also be tested.

Database	Spreadsheet	Word processing
Working with databases	**Working with cells and cell data**	*You should be familiar with a wide range of word processed business documents by now, e.g.*
■ Use primary and foreign keys	■ Cell formatting, including conditional formatting	■ Letters – multi-page and with tear-off slip
■ Create one-to-many relationships	■ Comments – add, edit, remove	■ Meetings – notice of meeting and agenda; minutes
■ Enforce referential integrity		■ Reports and Newsletters
■ Cascade updates and deletes	**Managing workbooks**	
■ Edit and delete relationships	■ Insert common data or formulae and formats simultaneously (linking or grouping worksheets)	*You should also be able to work with:*
■ Print database relationships		
	■ Insert page breaks	**Tables**
Queries		■ Embed data from a spreadsheet in a table with dynamic linkage
■ Criteria query on a minimum of two fields from multiple tables on full or partial text or values within fields (wildcards – * or ?)	**Data consolidation**	■ Convert text to table
	■ Summary worksheets/files using 3D references; pivot tables; pivot charts	■ Sort lists on up to three levels
■ Use AND, OR, NOT to join query criteria		■ Perform calculations – add, subtract, multiply and divide
■ Aggregate functions in queries e.g. sum, average, maximum and minimum	**Functions**	
■ Use a calculated field	■ Count IF	**Forms**
■ Sort on a minimum of two fields from multiple tables within query	■ Round	■ Create automatic form using form fields
	■ V and H look-ups	■ Work with drop-down list fields
■ Create a graph from a query		■ Work with check box fields
	Sorting	■ Protect a form
Forms	■ Filtering on two criteria	■ Delete form fields
■ Design fields	■ Grouping and outlining	
■ Establish order of data entry		**Working with document**
■ Set style and alignment	**Charts**	■ Create and delete footnotes and endnotes
■ Apply decorative enhancement	■ Customise data series in rows and columns	■ Modify content and positioning of existing footnotes and endnote
■ Insert header and footer		
■ Modify properties	**Importing data from external source**	■ Insert bookmarks and cross-references
■ Move, align, delete and edit objects on a form	■ Table from word processing document	■ Insert and delete section breaks
		■ Change page orientation in sections
■ Insert graphic	■ Data from a database table	■ Work with headers and footers across sections
		■ Format first page differently from other pages
Reports	**Exporting dynamically linked data**	■ Insert and delete comments and watermarks
■ Create a report from a table or query	■ Link spreadsheet data as a table and/or chart in a word processing document	■ Use, create and modify styles
■ Use calculations within a report – sum, average, minimum, maximum		■ Number sections and paragraphs
		■ Insert table of contents
■ Modify the layout of reports to ensure data is visible	**Print**	
	■ Completed worksheet/s and sections from worksheets in value and formulae view	**Mail merge**
■ Insert report header		■ Letters and labels using a word-processed data document or a database file
■ Insert page header or footer	■ Separate and embedded charts	
		Integration
Exporting data		■ Data from spreadsheet
■ Export data to spreadsheet or word processing software		■ Dynamically linked chart or graph from a spreadsheet
		■ Results of database queries
Print		**Print**
■ Extract/s from database		■ Complete document or part of document
■ Queries, forms and reports		

Before you start

Do your revision *before* you tackle this chapter – it may be better to use the sets of tasks as exam preparation and practice!

When you work through the practical paper for each set ensure that you:

- familiarise yourself with the files you will be using before you start – this is particularly important with the database question(s)
- read through the paper carefully and underline or highlight key instructions
- *always* read the *whole* question before you tackle it
- remember to include the reference and date on letters, even if it isn't on the exam question – at Higher you are expected to be familiar with letter layout. And watch out for enclosures – take time to read the letter content!
- make sure that the reference is on *every* print-out – it's usually given in the **Information for candidates** section
- read the **Information for candidates** section very carefully, as this may contain some important information not actually given in the question itself, such as the name of the person you are working for.

Database tips

- *Always* save your forms, queries and reports – even if the question doesn't tell you to. Give them sensible names – don't call them Form1, Query1, Report1, etc.
- When creating a database form, try the **AutoForm** option first – it will often get you off to a good start for the development of the form. If it doesn't look like AutoForm is giving you all the fields that you want, work through the **Form Wizard**, selecting the fields required.
- There may be some formatting required that is not explicitly asked for, for example, when inserting a picture into a form or report you may need to resize it so it displays correctly, or you may need to resize a text field or label to display all the data.
- When preparing a report under exam conditions, don't get tied down in the fine-tuning – especially instructions such as **ensure page breaks are in a suitable place**. You could spend a long time trying to get things to fit, when this aspect will be worth only one or two marks. Save the report and move on – you can come back to it later if you have time.

Spreadsheet tips

- When performing the same task on several worksheets at once, **group** the worksheets to save you time. However, remember that not all features work on grouped sheets, e.g. sort.
- If there aren't enough worksheets in your workbook, you'll have to add one.
- Make sure you use the correct **function** or **formula** – you won't get any marks for working out the answer in your head and then just typing it in.
- When printing out **formulas**, remember to display **gridlines** and **row and column headings** to help make your print-out easier to interpret, unless otherwise instructed.
- Use **Print Preview** to check that all information is visible before you print.
- If you have a **comment**, you will need to display it on your worksheet, or print it at the end of the sheet, to provide evidence that you have added one.
- If you are using the data in one cell in several formulas or functions, remember to use **absolute addressing**.

Word processing tips

- Watch out for things such as **Galashiels area** (see Set 1 of practice tasks). The new premises are in Galashiels, but the letter has to go to everyone in the **Galashiels area**, implying that there may be some records that don't just have Galashiels in the Town field.

- If you have a selective mail merge to do, you could set up a query in your database (if that is where the records come from) *or* do an advanced select in your word processing software.

- Label sizes – you may be asked to use any suitable label, or you may be given a particular label code. If given a code, remember that there are different lists that it might be in.

- You will need to put your reference on labels too.

- Labels can usually be produced using a database or word processing package.

- In reports, keep the layout consistent and watch the spacing above/below headings – it should be consistent throughout.

- Remember the **reference** – if there is no explicit instruction, put it in the usual place on a letter (above the date) or in the header or footer in a report.

> ### Hint
> Read through all these tips before you attempt each set of tasks.

Set 1

Information for candidates

You have recently joined **Caledonia IT Training** – an organisation that sells IT training courses and materials throughout the central belt of Scotland and the Borders.

You are responsible for maintaining the course booking database; sales records for books, learning materials and other items; organising courses and customer liaison.

Your boss is about to go off for a few days holiday, and has sent you some emails with details of a number of tasks she would like you to complete in her absence.

Read the emails carefully, and then carry out the tasks requested.

All documents should contain the reference **CalITT/*your initials***

You should complete all tasks within 1 hour and 20 minutes.

Email 1

From:	Joyce Smith, Director
To:	Administrative Assistant
Date:	Today's
Subject:	IT Training Database

1   **(a)** Please produce a list of all trainees that are booked on Word or Excel courses, regardless of level. I need a list of all those attending Word courses (at levels 1, 2 and 3) and those attending Excel courses (at levels 1, 2 and 3). You should display the list in ascending order on Course Title, and within each course the Surnames should be in ascending order. The Course Title, Trainee Surname and First Name, Job Title, Address and Email fields should be displayed in the result. Please print your results.

(b) Prepare a report showing details of the courses delivered by each trainer. Please view the information by Trainer, group the data by Venue, and sort the courses in ascending order by Title – display the Course Code, Course Title and Dates. Adjust the layout of the report if necessary to ensure that it fits on one page. The trainer data – code and name – should be on one row. The report should have today's date and page numbering in the footer. The report header should be *Courses delivered by Trainer* and the company logo should be displayed to the right of this header. Please print the report in portrait orientation.

Email 2

From:	Joyce Smith, Director
To:	Administrative Assistant
Date:	Today's
Subject:	Sales Date

1   Please update the January – March sales data file as follows:

(a) The data on each sheet should be sorted in ascending order by Media, and then in ascending order by Item. Also, swap the position of the Media and Item columns, and display the total income from all sales at the bottom of column E for each month. Print out the March worksheet, showing data and formulas.

(b) Prepare a 3D Pie Chart showing a percentage value of total sales for each month achieved over the 3 months. The chart title should be *Comparison of Total Sales*. Put the chart on a separate sheet and print it out with today's date in the footer area.

(c) Summarise the sales data for the 3 months onto a separate worksheet with links to the original data (ignore the total figures at the end of column E). The summary should show the total sales for each item over the 3 months. Put today's date and the reference in the footer and then print out the worksheet in Data and Formula view.

(d) Finally, for each month, provide information showing how many products sold 30 or more items each month. Print out results for March only (data and formulas).

2   **(a)** I have prepared a draft letter to be sent out to our customers inviting them to the opening of our new premises in Galashiels (filename – **New Premises Letter**). Please prepare a mail merge letter to all of the trainees we have had from the Galashiels area. Each letter should fit on one page. Please print the main document file and one of the result letters. Write a note on the print-out of the main document, stating how many result documents we have.

(b) I plan to email a form to other companies in the Borders. I have started work on it – in the file called **Form**. Please add appropriate fields to allow for online completion of the form. Most of the fields will be text fields. I want check boxes used at the Yes and No options, and a drop-down list for *If so, how did you hear of us?* giving the options as – Select an item: Scotsman; Glasgow Herald; Poster/Flyer; None of the above. Protect the form, then complete it with sample data and print it out so I can have a look at it.

Information for candidates

You work for your local bookshop – **Book Owl Bookshop** – a popular store that stocks a wide range of titles, which it sells through its retail outlet as well as over the internet.

As Personal Assistant to the shop manager, you have considerable responsibility and are sometimes left to cope when your manager is away.

Your manager has gone to a book fair for a few days and has left you in charge. He has also left you several tasks to complete before his return.

Company Name: Book Owl Bookshop

E-mail: info@bookowlbookshop.co.uk

Website: www.bookowlbookshop.co.uk

Read the emails carefully, and then carry out the tasks requested. You should complete all tasks within 1 hour and 20 minutes.

Each print-out should have the reference *Bookowl/your initials*

Email 1

From:	Jack Andrews, Store Manager
To:	Personal Assistant
Date:	Today's
Subject:	Book Owl Bookshop Database

1   We will be taking delivery of a large number of new books as a result of my trip. Please create a form for the Book table in the database as I think it will make it much easier for us to enter the details when we update our stock. Give the form a header – *Current Stock* – and format it to be size 18 and bold. Add the company logo to the form header area, and resize, format and/or move it as necessary to ensure it looks good. The author name should be displayed in one row, and all fields should be formatted to display all data/pictures fully. Print out the form showing the Castaways title, to give me an idea of how it will look.

2   **(a)** I need to know what the current value of our stock is. Could you work out the sales value of each book title – include the Category, Title, Author, Price, Number of Copies and Value of Stock (display the Value of Stock as currency).

(b) Display all of the data from the above task in a report. Group the data by Category, and sort the data into ascending order on Book Title. Summarise the data by calculating the total sale value of the books in each category, and also the total value of books in the whole report. Format the subtotals and total appropriately. Ensure that all data is displayed clearly, and try to ensure that the page breaks land in a sensible place. Print the last page of your report.

Email 2

From:	Jack Andrews, Store Manager
To:	Personal Assistant
Date:	Today's
Subject:	Poster and Invoice

1   Book sale – Cooking, Gardening, Crafts and Music – poster. Complete this and have it ready for me to proof when I get back. The shop will open from 9 am to 6 pm that day. Copy in a list of the books from the database. Just bring in the Title, Author, Original Price and Sale Price (this will be 50% of original price); format sale price to currency with 2 decimal places. Don't include the category.

   Make sure our logo is on the poster, and format it attractively to fit on one A4 page, portrait orientation. The books should be in ascending order on Price.

   Our company name, email and website details should be in the footer (Arial, size 10) – company name at the left margin and our email and website details at the right margin, on separate rows. Put a single top border above the footer. Print one copy for proofing.

2   Please run off some labels for the publishers. Use any suitable label layout. Sort the labels into ascending order by Publisher. Print them out.

3   I started working on an invoice layout – called **Draft Invoice**.

   Please finish this off by adding formulas and formatting as necessary, with the final layout fitting on one page, landscape orientation. I've put in some sample data to give you an idea of what it will contain – but set it up as if there are 12 items listed (rows 6 – 17).

   A discount is payable, depending on the value of the order: if the subtotal is £200 or more a 10% discount should be given, a subtotal between £100 and £199.99 gets a 5% discount, and a subtotal less than £100 gets no discount. Add a comment to the discount cell, explaining the calculation.

   We also need a formula to calculate the amount due.

   Adjust the column widths so that all data is displayed. Use text wrap in the column headings, adjust the font sizes and/or use bold/colour, etc. to make it look attractive. Format the numbers appropriately. Add our logo to the invoice.

   Can I have two print-outs of the final invoice please – one in Value and one in Formula view.

Information for candidates

You are employed as the **Student Record System Assistant** in the Student Records Office in your local college (Lockwood's Business College).

You are due to go on holiday this evening – and your boss has asked you to do a few tasks before you leave.

Read the emails carefully, and then carry out the tasks requested. You should complete all tasks within 1 hour and 20 minutes.

Each print-out should contain the reference **LBC/your initials**

Email 1

From:	Pedro Stephani, Studio Records Manager
To:	Student Record System Assistant
Date:	Today's
Subject:	Full-Time Statistics

1 Update the spreadsheet file that contains the full-time statistics. Add a comment to cell A1 stating where the data came from originally – the Student Record System.

Extract the data required, i.e. numbers on specific courses for the years requested and the average number of students per course, taking all courses and all years into account (display the average figure as a whole number). Highlight all course intakes that were less than 80% of the average intake figure.

Add a new row for 2008, showing the target figures (all courses are to increase their intake by 3). Format the worksheet effectively, and take two print-outs of the spreadsheet – one showing Values and the other showing Formulas. Ensure that the print-outs fit neatly onto the page(s) and are legible.

2 Prepare a column chart showing enrolments for each course for 2005–2007. The chart should be on a separate sheet. Give the chart a suitable title and use appropriate labels for the axes. The chart title should be size 16, and use a pattern or other effect on the 2005 series. Print the chart out.

Email 2

From:	Pedro Stephani, Studio Records Manager
To:	Student Record System Assistant
Date:	Today's
Subject:	Annual Report

Complete the Annual Report for me please, following the guidelines below. Use a watermark to indicate that they are still in draft.

1. The top two lines of text on page 1 should be on a Title Page – format effectively. The college logo should also be on the title page.

2. The Normal style should be modified to Arial, size 12.
   Format Range of Courses, Enrolment Data, Future Developments, Student Success Stories and Next Year's Calendar with the Heading 1 style (which should be Arial, size 14 and bold).
   Format the student names under the Student Success Stories heading using Heading 2 style (Arial, size 13 and bold).
   Make sure that the spacing between the headings/paragraphs is consistent throughout, and fully justify the text throughout (except for the title page).

3. The data from the spreadsheet file on **Full-Time Enrolments**, for years 1996 through to 2007, should be copied into the report where indicated (remove the conditional formatting from the cells in the report). The data should be presented in landscape orientation (although the rest of the report should be portrait). Adjust the font size within the table to 12 if necessary, and resize the columns, etc. to ensure that the table fits well on the page.

4. Add square bullets to the lists in the Future Developments section.

5. Tidy up the table for Next Year's Calendar – display the content in two columns and format it effectively.

6. Add page numbering and today's date to the footer of each page except the title page. Ensure that the page number is centred and the date is at the right margin on each page. Add a top border to the footer on each page.

7. Add a Table of Contents to page 2.

8. Print the report.

Email 3

From:	Pedro Stephani, Studio Records Manager
To:	Student Record System Assistant
Date:	Today's
Subject:	Student Records Database

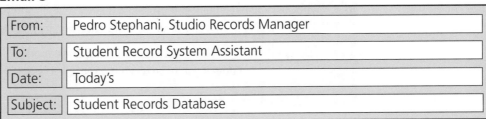

1. I have a meeting next week to discuss course enrolments for next year. Please print out details of how many enrolments we have on each course so far. I just need a brief summary – Course Code, Course Title and Number of Enrolments will do. Sort the data in descending order on Number of Enrolments.

2. Prepare a report (landscape orientation) to send through to Student Welfare Services listing all students that are enrolled on each course. They need all the contact details for each student.
   Display the data under Mode of Attendance, with the Course Code and Course Title on one row under this. The student data should be sorted into ascending order on Surname and then First Name. Put the college logo in the report header, your name in the page footer, and adjust the page breaks if necessary so that they are in a sensible place. Ensure that all the contact data is clearly visible. Give the report a suitable name.

Email 1

1 (a)

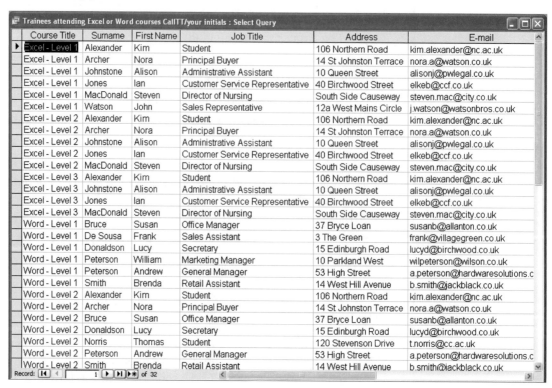

Hints

- You should use **wildcards** in your criteria – an asterisk (*) to represent a string of characters, or a question mark (?) to represent an individual character.

- When performing a multi-level sort in a query, the main sort field e.g. Course Title in this example, must be to the *left* of the secondary sort field (Surname).

- The query name will print out in the heading on your print-out, so the marker will know if you have given it a sensible name or not.

Database Query		
Evidence	**Marks**	**Comments**
List showing trainees on Word and Excel courses only (Word* or Excel*)	2	There should be 32 records.
Sorted on Course Title, and then Surname, Ascending Order	1	No mark if sorted incorrectly.
Course Title, Trainee Surname, First Name, Job Title, Address and Email fields present	1	No mark if all fields are not present and displayed fully.
Query has suitable name	1	No mark if saved as Query 1.
CalITT/your initials evident	1	In query name on this example.
Total marks	**6**	

1 (b)

Your results may look slightly different if you have used different formatting options.

The reference is in the footer in this example – the most logical place for it – but would have been accepted in any position.

You may need to move fields or resize them to display all data fully.

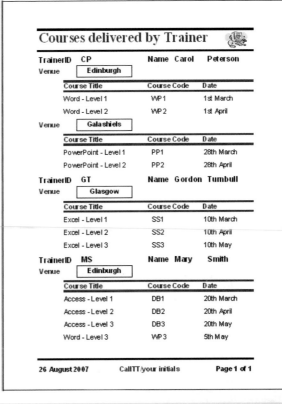

Hints

- Use the **Label** tool to insert an object for the reference and your name or initials.
- Double-click on an object, e.g. picture or label, to display its **Properties**.
- To display the picture properly, you will need to set the **Size Mode** property to **Stretch** or **Zoom**. This can be done using the **Format** or **All** tab in the **Object Properties**.

Database Report		
Evidence	**Marks**	**Comments**
Report showing courses by Trainer	1	
Trainer ID and name on one row	1	You will need to move, and perhaps resize, the fields.
Grouped by Venue	1	Evidenced in Carol Peterson data.
Sorted in ascending order by Title	1	
Course Code, Course Title and Dates fields present	1	No mark if all fields not present or field contents not fully visible.
Today's date and page numbering in footer	1	No mark if either is missing.
Header – **Courses delivered by Trainer**	1	No mark if incorrect header or header not fully displayed.
Company logo	1	No mark if logo not present or not displayed properly.
Printed portrait orientation, on one page	1	No mark given if all layout instructions aren't followed.
CalITT/your initials	1	Must be somewhere on report – footer in this example.
Total marks	**10**	

Email 2

1 (a)

March Sales Summary

Media	Item	Value	Number Sold	Total
Book	Access in Easy Steps	£ 12.50	44	£ 550.00
Book	Advanced Access	£ 15.00	14	£ 210.00
Book	Advanced Excel	£ 15.00	16	£ 240.00
Book	Advanced PowerPoint	£ 15.00	20	£ 300.00
Book	Advanced Word	£ 15.00	14	£ 210.00
Book	Excel in Easy Steps	£ 12.50	42	£ 525.00
Book	PowerPoint in Easy Steps	£ 12.50	37	£ 462.50
Book	Borders - Screensaver & Pictures	£ 10.00	14	£ 140.00
DVD	Edinburgh - Screensaver & Pictures	£ 10.00	45	£ 450.00
DVD	Glasgow - Screensaver & Pictures	£ 10.00	38	£ 380.00
...ss - CBT	£ 45.00	25	£ 1,125.00
...l - CBT	£ 45.00	14	£ 630.00
...erPoint - CBT	£ 45.00	26	£ 1,170.00
...d - CBT	£ 45.00	52	£ 2,340.00
...ensaver & Pictures	£ 10.00	22	£ 220.00
...ard Shortcuts	£ 5.00	15	£ 75.00
...rd Shortcuts	£ 5.00	15	£ 75.00
...eyboard Shortcuts	£ 5.00	15	£ 75.00
...rd Shortcuts	£ 5.00	15	£ 75.00
£ 6.50	8	£ 52.00
£ 6.50	33	£ 214.50
£ 6.50	42	£ 273.00
£ 6.50	28	£ 182.00
£ 4.00	2	£ 8.00
£ 4.00	25	£ 100.00
£ 4.00	28	£ 112.00
£ 4.00	21	£ 84.00
...ard Shortcuts	£ 3.40	20	£ 68.00
...rd Shortcuts	£ 3.40	20	£ 68.00
...eyboard Shortcuts	£ 3.40	20	£ 68.00
...rd Shortcuts	£ 3.40	20	£ 68.00

£ 10,962.50

March Sales Summary

	A (Media)	B (Item)	C (Value)	D (Number Sold)	E (Total)
3	Media	Item	Value	Number Sold	Total
4	Book	Access in Easy Steps	12.5	44	=C4*D4
5	Book	Advanced Access	15	14	=C5*D5
6	Book	Advanced Excel	15	16	=C6*D6
7	Book	Advanced PowerPoint	15	20	=C7*D7
8	Book	Advanced Word	15	14	=C8*D8
9	Book	Excel in Easy Steps	12.5	42	=C9*D9
10	Book	PowerPoint in Easy Steps	12.5	37	=C10*D10
11	Book	Word in Easy Steps	12.5	33	=C11*D11
12	DVD	Borders - Screensaver & Pictures	10	14	=C12*D12
13	DVD	Edinburgh - Screensaver & Pictures	10	45	=C13*D13
14	DVD	Glasgow - Screensaver & Pictures	10	38	=C14*D14
15	DVD	Learning Access - CBT	45	25	=C15*D15
16	DVD	Learning Excel - CBT	45	14	=C16*D16
17	DVD	Learning PowerPoint - CBT	45	26	=C17*D17
18	DVD	Learning Word - CBT	45	52	=C18*D18
19	DVD	Stirling - Screensaver & Pictures	10	22	=C19*D19
20	Leaflet (10)	Access Keyboard Shortcuts	5	15	=C20*D20
21	Leaflet (10)	Excel Keyboard Shortcuts	5	15	=C21*D21
22	Leaflet (10)	PowerPoint Keyboard Shortcuts	5	15	=C22*D22
23	Leaflet (10)	Word Keyboard Shortcuts	5	15	=C23*D23
24	Mousemat	Borders	6.5	8	=C24*D24
25	Mousemat	Edinburgh	6.5	33	=C25*D25
26	Mousemat	Glasgow	6.5	42	=C26*D26
27	Mousemat	Stirling	6.5	28	=C27*D27
28	Mug	Borders	4	2	=C28*D28
29	Mug	Edinburgh	4	25	=C29*D29
30	Mug	Glasgow	4	28	=C30*D30
31	Mug	Stirling	4	21	=C31*D31
32	Poster	Access Keyboard Shortcuts	3.4	20	=C32*D32
33	Poster	Excel Keyboard Shortcuts	3.4	20	=C33*D33
34	Poster	PowerPoint Keyboard Shortcuts	3.4	20	=C34*D34
35	Poster	Word Keyboard Shortcuts	3.4	20	=C35*D35
36					
37					=SUM(E4:E36)

Hints

■ In a multilevel sort, choose **Sort** from the **Data** menu and then specify your sort options in the dialog box.

■ **Moving columns or rows:** When moving (or copying) columns or rows, be careful that you don't replace the data occupying the destination cells.
Either:
– insert a blank column or row where you want to move or copy the cells to
– cut (or copy) the data
– paste into the empty cells
Or:
– cut (or copy) the data required
– select the top left cell in the area that you want to move or copy the data to
– open the insert menu and choose Cut cells (or Copied cells)

■ **Grouping and ungrouping**
– To group adjacent worksheets, click on the sheet tab of the first one you wish to group, and then hold the [Shift] key down and click on the sheet tab of the last sheet you wish to group.
– To group non-adjacent worksheets, click on the sheet tab of the first one and then hold down [Ctrl] as you click on each of the other sheet tabs required.
– To Ungroup your worksheets, either *left-click* on any sheet tab that is not part of the group or *right-click* on a sheet tab and choose **Ungroup Sheets** from the pop-up menu.

Spreadsheet task – over multiple sheets		
Evidence	**Marks**	**Comments**
Data sorted by Media, and then by Item	2	No marks if both columns not sorted.
Swap position of Media and Item columns	2	This can be done with sheets grouped.
Total income at bottom of column E on all sheets	1	This can be done with sheets grouped.
Total marks	**5**	

1 (b)

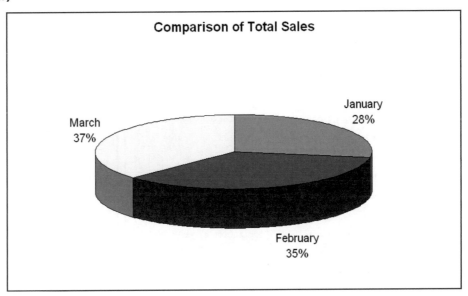

Comparison of Total Sales

January 28%

March 37%

February 35%

Hints

■ Remember to put in your reference and/or initials, even if it isn't explicitly asked for in the question. The **Instructions for candidates** will have told you what is required.

Charting		
Evidence	**Marks**	**Comments**
Correct data laid out appropriately for charting purposes	1	Data could be displayed anywhere on worksheet.
3D Pie Chart showing percentage value of total sales for each month	2	Lose 1 mark if chart not 3D pie chart; lose 1 mark if percentages not given.
Legend or data labels showing months need to be present	1	As no explicit instruction given, either acceptable, but not both.
Chart on separate sheet	1	
Chart title – **Comparison of Total Sales**	1	No mark if title incorrect.
Today's date in footer	1	No mark if not given.
Printed	1	
Total marks	**8**	

1 (c)

Sales Summary January - March

Media	Item	Value	Number Sold	Total
Book	Access in Easy Steps	£ 12.50	112	£1,400.00
Book	Advanced Access	£ 15.00	78	£1,170.00
Book	Advanced Excel	£ 15.00	46	£ 690.00
Book	Advanced PowerPoint	£ 15.00	75	£1,125.00
Book	Advanced Word	£ 15.00	35	£ 525.00
Book	Excel in Easy Steps	£ 12.50	86	£1,075.00
	PowerPoint in Easy Steps	£ 12.50	73	£ 912.50
	Word in Easy Steps	£ 12.50	95	£1,187.50
	Borders - Screensaver & Pictures	£ 10.00	58	£ 580.00
	Edinburgh - Screensaver & Pictures	£ 10.00	133	£1,330.00
	Glasgow - Screensaver & Pictures	£ 10.00	78	£ 780.00
	Learning Access - CBT	£ 45.00	85	£3,825.00
	Learning Excel - CBT	£ 45.00	39	£1,755.00
	Learning PowerPoint - CBT	£ 45.00	60	£2,700.00
	Learning Word - CBT	£ 45.00	117	£5,265.00
	Stirling - Screensaver & Pictures	£ 10.00	51	£ 510.00
	Access Keyboard Shortcuts	£ 5.00	50	£ 250.00
	Excel Keyboard Shortcuts	£ 5.00	49	£ 245.00
	PowerPoint Keyboard Shortcuts	£ 5.00	49	£ 245.00
	Word Keyboard Shortcuts	£ 5.00	55	£ 275.00
	Borders	£ 6.50	26	£ 169.00
	Edinburgh	£ 6.50	139	£ 903.50
	Glasgow	£ 6.50	117	£ 760.50
	Stirling	£ 6.50	82	£ 533.00
	Borders	£ 4.00	15	£ 60.00
	Edinburgh	£ 4.00	120	£ 480.00
	Glasgow	£ 4.00	91	£ 364.00
	Stirling	£ 4.00	47	£ 188.00
	Access Keyboard Shortcuts	£ 3.40	28	£ 95.20
	Excel Keyboard Shortcuts	£ 3.40	26	£ 88.40
	PowerPoint Keyboard Shortcuts	£ 3.40	29	£ 98.60
	Word Keyboard Shortcuts	£ 3.40	29	£ 98.60

/your initials *Today's date*

Sales Summary January - March

	A	B	C	D	E
1		Sales Summary January - March			
2					
3	Media	Item	Value	Number Sold	Total
7	Book	Access in Easy Steps	12.5	=SUM(D4:D6)	=SUM(E4:E6)
11	Book	Advanced Access	15	=SUM(D8:D10)	=SUM(E8:E10)
15	Book	Advanced Excel	15	=SUM(D12:D14)	=SUM(E12:E14)
19	Book	Advanced PowerPoint	15	=SUM(D16:D18)	=SUM(E16:E18)
23	Book	Advanced Word	15	=SUM(D20:D22)	=SUM(E20:E22)
27	Book	Excel in Easy Steps	12.5	=SUM(D24:D26)	=SUM(E24:E26)
31	Book	PowerPoint in Easy Steps	12.5	=SUM(D28:D30)	=SUM(E28:E30)
35	Book	Word in Easy Steps	12.5	=SUM(D32:D34)	=SUM(E32:E34)
39	DVD	Borders - Screensaver & Pictures	10	=SUM(D36:D38)	=SUM(E36:E38)
43	DVD	Edinburgh - Screensaver & Pictures	10	=SUM(D40:D42)	=SUM(E40:E42)
47	DVD	Glasgow - Screensaver & Pictures	10	=SUM(D44:D46)	=SUM(E44:E46)
51	DVD	Learning Access - CBT	45	=SUM(D48:D50)	=SUM(E48:E50)
55	DVD	Learning Excel - CBT	45	=SUM(D52:D54)	=SUM(E52:E54)
59	DVD	Learning PowerPoint - CBT	45	=SUM(D56:D58)	=SUM(E56:E58)
63	DVD	Learning Word - CBT	45	=SUM(D60:D62)	=SUM(E60:E62)
67	DVD	Stirling - Screensaver & Pictures	10	=SUM(D64:D66)	=SUM(E64:E66)
71	Leaflet (10)	Access Keyboard Shortcuts	5	=SUM(D68:D70)	=SUM(E68:E70)
75	Leaflet (10)	Excel Keyboard Shortcuts	5	=SUM(D72:D74)	=SUM(E72:E74)
79	Leaflet (10)	PowerPoint Keyboard Shortcuts	5	=SUM(D76:D78)	=SUM(E76:E78)
83	Leaflet (10)	Word Keyboard Shortcuts	5	=SUM(D80:D82)	=SUM(E80:E82)
87	Mousemat	Borders	6.5	=SUM(D84:D86)	=SUM(E84:E86)
91	Mousemat	Edinburgh	6.5	=SUM(D88:D90)	=SUM(E88:E90)
95	Mousemat	Glasgow	6.5	=SUM(D92:D94)	=SUM(E92:E94)
99	Mousemat	Stirling	6.5	=SUM(D96:D98)	=SUM(E96:E98)
103	Mug	Borders	4	=SUM(D100:D102)	=SUM(E100:E102)
107	Mug	Edinburgh	4	=SUM(D104:D106)	=SUM(E104:E106)
111	Mug	Glasgow	4	=SUM(D108:D110)	=SUM(E108:E110)
115	Mug	Stirling	4	=SUM(D112:D114)	=SUM(E112:E114)
119	Poster	Access Keyboard Shortcuts	3.4	=SUM(D116:D118)	=SUM(E116:E118)
123	Poster	Excel Keyboard Shortcuts	3.4	=SUM(D120:D122)	=SUM(E120:E122)
127	Poster	PowerPoint Keyboard Shortcuts	3.4	=SUM(D124:D126)	=SUM(E124:E126)
131	Poster	Word Keyboard Shortcuts	3.4	=SUM(D128:D130)	=SUM(E128:E130)

CallTT/your initials *Today's date*

Hints

■ To add a worksheet, *right-click* on a sheet tab and choose **Insert…** from the pop-up menu. The new worksheet will be inserted to the left of the sheet tab you right-click on. If you want to move the worksheet to a different position you, drag and drop the sheet tab.

Consolidation

Evidence	Marks	Comments
Data consolidated on to separate sheet with links	2	Lose 1 mark if on same worksheet. Any consolidation method is acceptable, e.g. data consolidation or using cell references.
Give consolidated data a sensible title	1	Use your initiative here – it isn't explicitly asked for, but things don't make sense unless you do this.
Total figures ignored	1	That is, the total at the bottom of column E.
Footer	1	Date and reference present.
Two print-outs – Data and Formulas	1	Show all data. Each fitted on 1 page.
Total marks	**6**	

1 (d)

22 Leaflet (10)	PowerPoint Keyboard Shortcuts	5	15	=C22*D22
23 Leaflet (10)	Word Keyboard Shortcuts	5	15	=C23*D23
24 Mousemat	Borders	6.5	8	=C24*D24
25 Mousemat	Edinburgh	6.5	33	=C25*D25
26 Mousemat	Glasgow	6.5	42	=C26*D26
27 Mousemat	Stirling	6.5	28	=C27*D27
28 Mug	Borders	4	2	=C28*D28
29 Mug	Edinburgh	4	25	=C29*D29
30 Mug	Glasgow	4	28	=C30*D30
31 Mug	Stirling	4	21	=C31*D31
32 Poster	Access Keyboard Shortcuts	3.4	20	=C32*D32
33 Poster	Excel Keyboard Shortcuts	3.4	20	=C33*D33
34 Poster	PowerPoint Keyboard Shortcuts	3.4	20	=C34*D34
35 Poster	Word Keyboard Shortcuts	3.4	20	=C35*D35
36				
37	Number of products selling more than 30 items		=COUNTIF(D4:D35,">=30")	=SUM(E4:E36)

The screenshot above shows just the formulas that are important in this task. The CountIF value for March should be 9.

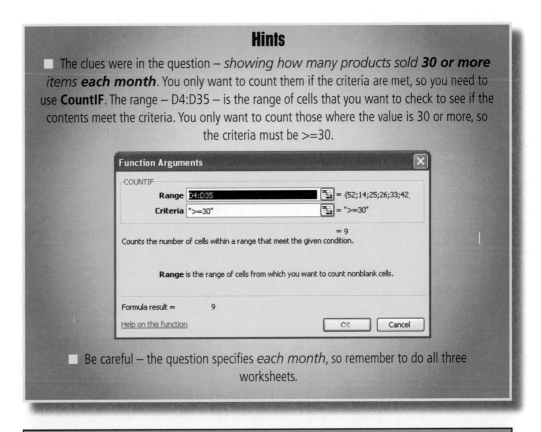

Hints

■ The clues were in the question – *showing how many products sold **30 or more** items **each month***. You only want to count them if the criteria are met, so you need to use **CountIF**. The range – D4:D35 – is the range of cells that you want to check to see if the contents meet the criteria. You only want to count those where the value is 30 or more, so the criteria must be >=30.

■ Be careful – the question specifies *each month*, so remember to do all three worksheets.

Sales >=30		
Evidence	**Marks**	**Comments**
CountIF function used	1	No mark if CountIF is not used.
Range identified correctly	1	Must use CountIF to get this mark.
Criteria set correctly – products >= 30 items sold	1	Must use CountIF to get this mark.
Above on all three sheets	1	You could have grouped the sheets to do this.
Print-out of March showing formulae and values, each print-out fitting on 1 sheet	1	Make sure that *CalITT/your initials* is on the print-out. The formula print-out should have grid lines and row/column labels displayed.
Total marks	**5**	

2 (a)

Caledonia IT Training
24 St Johns Street
EDINBURGH
EH3 1ZZ
Telephone: 0131 444 1010
E-mail: info@caledoniaitt.co.uk

CalITT/your initials

5 April 200X

«Title» «First_Name» «Surname»
«Job_Title»
«Company_Name»
«Town»
«Postcode»

Dear «First_Name»

OPEN DAY AT CALEDONIA IT TRAINING – 30 June

It is with great pleasure that I write to invite you to the opening of our new premises at 47 Bank Street, Galashiels.

Please email to confirm your attendance, stating how many will be in your group. We look forward to seeing you on the 30 June.

Yours sincerely

Joyce Smith
Director

Enc

Hints

- Use your letter **house style** when producing a letter. You *must* have the **reference** and **date**. Then it is usually the inside address and salutation.

- Complimentary close – use **Yours sincerely** if you have used the name of the person you are sending the letter to in the salutation, e.g. Dear Peter or Dear Mrs Jones, or **Yours faithfully** if your salutation is Dear Sir or Dear Madam.

- Read the letter to check for any enclosures and remember to put **Enc** or **Encs** at the end if necessary.

Word processing task – Mail merge		
Evidence	**Marks**	**Comments**
Merge document set up as letter	2	Use house style for reference. Use complimentary close.
Main document linked to data document	1	
Correct fields inserted	3	Lose 1 mark for each field not inserted – max. 3 marks.
Galashiels area targeted	2	Result document should have 4 letters.
Reference, complimentary close and Enc present	2	Lose 1 mark for each omission – max. 2 marks. Lose 1 mark if incorrect complimentary close used. Reference – CalITT/your initials or JS/your initials are acceptable.
Each letter fits on 1 page	1	You may need to adjust formatting, e.g. font size/spacing/margins.
Total marks	**11**	

2 (b)

Caledonia IT Training
24 St Johns Street
EDINBURGH
EH3 1ZZ

Telephone: 0131 444 1010
E-mail: info@caledoniaitt.co.uk

CalITT/your initials

OPEN DAY AT CALEDONIA IT TRAINING – 30 June: 3.00 – 7.00 pm

It is with great pleasure that I write to invite you to the opening of our new premises at 47 Bank Street, Galashiels.

The premises will have 2 training rooms, each with 6 brand new PCs with a wide range of business and web design software.

You will have an opportunity see our facilities, speak to our training consultants and also meet existing customers from the Galashiels area. There will also be a buffet and drinks – so do come along and help us celebrate.

If you would like to join us, please complete the form below and return it to the above address, indicating how many will be attending on 30 June.

First Name Jennifer   Surname Brotherstone

Job Title   Supplies Manager

Company   Peter Watson plc

Telephone No 01896 222 111   E-mail   jenbroth@pwatson.co.uk

Have you heard of our training company before? Yes ☒   No ☐

If so, how did you hear of us?   Scotsman

How many will be attending?   3

We look forward to meeting you.

Joyce Smith

Director

Hints

- Display the **Forms** toolbar to help you to add fields to your form – **View, Toolbars, Forms**.

- **Double-click** on a form field to display its properties so that you can specify any options required, or select the form field and then click **Form Field Options** on the Forms toolbar.

Word processing task – form

Evidence	Marks	Comments
Text fields added	3	First Name, Surname, Job Title, Company, Tel No, Email, How many will be attending. Lose 1 mark for any missed, max. 3 marks.
Check boxes (x2)	1	Yes and No – no mark if both not done.
Drop-down list	2	How did you hear of us?
Form protected	1	Evidenced by form being completed.
Form completed	1	Details in every field – fully visible.
Form printed	1	Reference must be somewhere on form.
Total marks	**9**	

Total marks for Set 1	**60 marks**

Remember

Suggested solutions to practice task sets 2 and 3 are on the Leckie and Leckie website.
Go to: **www.leckieandleckie.co.uk** and then click on the Learning Lab button.
Navigate to the Higher Administration Course Notes page.

ANSWERS TO QUICK QUESTIONS

1 Effectiveness in the workplace

Quick Questions 1

1 Senior administrator will supervise and delegate work; junior administrator will follow procedures and work as a member of a team.

2 Reception duties; keeping records; presenting information; dealing with customers; handling information; storing and retrieving information.

3 Self-motivated and enthusiastic; good communication skills; can use initiative; positive attitude.

4 Essential: the successful candidate must have the specified quality or qualification, e.g. a Higher Grade Administration. Desirable: the successful candidate will find it helpful if they have the specified skill or quality, e.g. speaking a second language.

5 The process of analysing the purpose and duties of a job role and matching these to the current requirements of the organisation. Nowadays it is less likely that when a vacancy arises a post will automatically be replaced.

Quick Questions 2

1 Examples include: priorities list – breaks down tasks into an order in which they need to be completed; action plan – breaks down tasks into jobs, who is to do them and by when; electronic diary.

2 A PDP is a formal document which records the aims and objectives that need to be met by the employee through training or development. Usually completed prior to an annual review or appraisal.

3 Reasons given for not getting jobs done, e.g. telephone interruptions, not delegating tasks, dealing with visitors, meetings taking longer than necessary.

4 By setting up regular meetings with staff to check how well the work is progressing; using a Gantt Chart to record milestones.

5 A target or goal which can be quantified and for which evidence can be produced.

Quick Questions 3

1 Work well together and support each other; help make decisions; take on responsibility for set tasks; being prepared to negotiate and compromise; giving feedback and contributing to meetings.

2 Performing – this is when the team is working together towards common aims and goals.

3 Personality clashes between team members; changing expectations from some members; lack of resources.

4 Someone with good social skills (people person); someone who can communicate and organise, delegate and motivate.

5 As appropriate, e.g. the Checker – because I like things to be correct.

Quick Questions 1

1 **a** Career break: advantages to employee include allowing a good work–life balance, e.g. family and career; advantages to employer include being able to retain valuable staff.

b Flexi-time: advantages to employee include flexibility in planning time around personal life; advantages to employer include less time lost to medical appointments.

2 An employer will outsource work when the supply of labour is cheaper or more skilled than their own workforce.

3 Hot-desking saves space, reducing rent costs for employers and the costs of providing workstations for all employees.

4 Employer may use a fixed-term contract at Christmas to cover holiday period, but a temporary contract if an employee is off sick and they are not sure when they will be back to work.

5 An implied term is one that it is reasonable to expect, for example, that the employer will provide adequate resources for the employee to carry out their job.

Quick Questions 2

1 More sociable; better communication between staff.

2 Sick building syndrome is when staff complain of illnesses which they feel are associated with the building, e.g. headaches and sore throats.

3 Space, equipment, décor, acoustics.

4 Ergonomics has highlighted the importance of matching people to their environment and being aware of how they sit at desks and use equipment in their working lives.

5 Newsletters, meetings.

3 Recruiting, developing and supporting staff

Quick Questions 1

1 Helps to identify and determine exact requirements of a job.

2 Used to determine personality traits and problem solving abilities of prospective candidates.

3 To comply with equal opportunities legislation which makes it illegal to discriminate on the grounds of race, sex, age, religion, etc.

4 One to one – one interviewer and one interviewee; a first informal interview, followed by a more formal one; interviewed in front of a panel, possibly requiring a presentation.

5 To ensure candidate is telling the truth and that there are no issues or surprises for the new employer.

Quick Questions 2

1 To identify and match business and personal objectives; to discover work potential of employees especially with regards to promotion; to identify training needs; to control and monitor performance; to assist individuals with their own self-development.

2 Steps are: further training; appraisal interview, examine work role; discuss and set targets; complete forms; agree performance criteria; complete personal

development plan; measure actual performance against criteria; salary review and/or bonus.

3   Education: process of giving employee background academic knowledge to undertake job (e.g. a degree). Training: process of gaining knowledge and skills to do current job. Development: process of identifying future potential and undertaking either education or training to achieve it.

4   To show their commitment to training and continual professional development; it also gives them a standard to show what they are working towards.

5   On-the-job: demonstrations, job rotation, coaching from a mentor, working on a specific project. Off-the-job: lectures, online learning, case studies, individual projects, in-tray exercises.

Quick Questions 3

1   Loss of motivation; loss of commitment; unable to cope with workload; more aggressive and argumentative.

2   It saves time and money and helps avoid a breakdown in communication and relationships.

3   Advice, Conciliation and Arbitration Service – an independent body which helps to mediate in industrial disputes.

4   Keep in touch with employee; discuss their return to work and how it should be phased; if this does not work, take disciplinary action.

5   Organisations realise that a healthier and happier workforce will be more productive and better motivated.

4   Meetings

Quick Questions 1

1   To discuss and generate ideas; to motivate and team build; to set targets and agree objectives; to plan and make decisions.

2   It is the informal method of communication that exists within organisations, often mainly office gossip. Information can be communicated faster than by more formal routes.

3   Executive; Advisory; Joint; Standing; Ad hoc; Sub-committee.

4   Starts and finishes meeting; keeps control; makes decisions; signs minutes.

5   Plan carefully and state purpose; prepare agenda and send out before the meeting; set a time limit for the meeting; delegate responsibilities; follow up actions.

Quick Questions 2

1   Agenda is a programme to follow during the meeting, so helps control the meeting; minutes are a record of what took place, so can be referred to at a later date.

2   Specify exactly what is required, when and where; take dietary requirements into account; always include water.

3   Apologies for absence; minutes of previous meeting; matters arising; any other business; date of next meeting.

4   Formal minutes: record more details of what was said at the meeting and the resulting action that needs to be taken. Action minutes: these are more like notes and only record what has to be done, by when and by whom.

5   The chairperson in consultation with the secretary.

Quick Questions 3

1 It is the minimum number of people who must be present before a meeting can legally take place.

2 Proposed; seconded; voted; if passed, becomes a resolution.

3 It is used by the chairperson if there are an equal number of votes for and against a motion in order that a decision can be made.

4 Paper diary involves contacting individual participants and asking them if they are free to make the meeting, whereas electronic diary allows secretary to access all diaries electronically to find a time convenient for all participants, then send an email seeking confirmation – if the date is accepted then an entry is automatically placed in the diary and a reminder sent nearer the time.

5 Networks have allowed the use of discussion groups, instant messaging, webcams and blogs.

5 Effective customer service

Quick Questions 1

1 Vision: how management sees the business growing and developing. Mission statement: a slogan or catchphrase which illustrates this vision.

2 It will ensure the quality of its customer care; measure and test that customer needs are satisfied; put service level agreements in place; deal with customer complaints.

3 Increased sales; customer satisfaction; a good reputation.

4 Competent; confident; courteous.

5 Demoralised and demotivated staff; loss of reputation; loss of standing and status in the market place; loss of customers; reduced profit.

Quick Questions 2

1 Any three of: develop a customer satisfaction survey; create an internal newsletter; create special customer awards; provide warranties and guarantees.

2 They give confidence in the organisation and its products and services; money back if unsatisfied; repairs or replacements at no extra cost.

3 Questionnaire; telephone survey; online survey; face-to-face interview; customer focus group.

4 Encourages customers to use the same shop over and over again for loyalty points and gifts; the organisation can use the card to obtain valuable statistics on customer buying habits.

5 Any three of: don't want to make a fuss/cause unpleasantness; didn't make any difference the last time/don't think it will make a difference; too scared of assistants; takes too much time; don't know whom to complain to.

6 The role of information in decision making

Quick Questions 1

1 Data: raw facts and figures that have been collected for some purpose. Information: data that has been processed in some way, to add some meaning to it so that it can be used to help make decisions.

2 Any four of: *collect*, e.g. from email, sales figures, company documents etc.; *check* – that you have the correct data; *organise* – sort it or group it; *analyse* – perform calculations or extract data from it; *store* – electronically or in manual files; *distribute* – via email, internet, mail service, courier, etc.

3 Internal sources: company reports giving details of company progress and future developments; minutes of meetings recording what has been agreed at meetings and what actions need to be taken; financial records showing details of sales and purchases. External sources: government papers outlining legislation; suppliers' price lists; trade magazine articles giving information on developments in your area/specialism.

4 Quantitative information: can be counted or measured, e.g. sales figures or exam marks. It is usually presented numerically. Organisations can use it to help them analyse information, spot trends and make forecasts. Qualitative information: usually expressed in words and is used to give opinions or judgements. Companies often use it when carrying out customer satisfaction surveys, e.g. getting feedback from customers who have stayed at their hotel. It can be biased, and difficult to analyse.

5 Advantages: evidence of what has been discussed/agreed; you can refer back to it. Disadvantages: it takes time to produce so may be out of date by the time you get it; it may be difficult to get something clarified.

Quick Questions 2

1 **a, d, g**   Strategic   **b, e, f**   Tactical   **c**   Operational

2 Any six of: accurate; up to date; concise; timely; cost effective; relevant; objective; clear; complete; objective.

3 Scope: refers to the extent to which a decision affects an organisation. Strategic level decisions affect the organisation as a whole and will do so for the longer term. Tactical level decisions affect functional areas in the medium term as steps are taken to implement the strategic plans. Operational level decisions are the day-to-day decisions taken to ensure shifts are covered, production runs smoothly and targets are met.

4 Strategic: company director or chairman. Tactical: middle level management/ departmental managers. Operational: shift supervisor, office manager.

5 Any one of: easy to make errors; not always easy to interpret; the message can get lost in the detail.

7   The impact of ICT on work practices and management of information

Quick Questions 1

1 Any one of: Input: only need to enter data once, which speeds up data entry, and makes it easier to ensure data is accurate; data can be input in a variety of ways – keyed in, scanned in, OCR; validity checks can be used to help ensure data entry is accurate. Processing: data can be processed faster; data can be processed to produce different outputs for different purposes; fewer staff are required to process the data. Output: output can be in range of formats, e.g. table, graph; output can be sent to different output/distribution devices, e.g. printer, PDA, email, website; easy to use standard templates/layouts so staff and customers know where to find the information they require.

2 Information to be input can be sent electronically, or collected from electronic forms – no paper necessary. Output does not need to be printed, e.g. can be sent via email and stored electronically.

Quick Questions 2

1 Any three of: text boxes, check boxes, radio buttons, combo boxes (drop-down lists), list boxes.

2 Any three of: staff can access database at same time; all data held centrally in one place – so everyone uses the same data; access rights can be controlled to ensure appropriate levels of access, e.g. read write, read only or no access; easier to maintain the data and keep it up to date; input checks e.g. validation checks can be used to help ensure data entered accurately.

3 Any two of: email, fax, internet, mobile phone, pager, etc.

4 Advantages include: internal email; access to centralised files and databases; cost savings on peripherals, e.g. printers. Disadvantages include: expense and effort to set up; specialist staff necessary; if network goes down, work effectively stops.

5 Benefits include: potential to reach global market; shop open 24/7; potential savings on premises and staff.

Quick Questions 3

1 Any two of: staff may feel isolated; problems with communication between home workers and office; some staff may have difficulty working away from office base – may not be able to stay focused/disciplined to get work done; possible problems ensuring health and safety issues implemented or data security procedures followed.

2 Desk sharing – staff do not have their own desk, but use whatever desk is available when they are in the office. They may have to book a desk when they need one.

3 Any three of: improved networks so staff can access company files from anywhere with a computer and a suitable network connection; secure internet connections reduce the chance of data being intercepted by unauthorised users; speed at which data can be transferred via email and the internet to staff working off-site; drive of environmentally friendly policies – reducing commuting and therefore pollution; desire of staff to have a better work–life balance.

Quick Questions 4

1 Data management refers to the systems, procedures and controls that relate to the way data is input, stored and retrieved. It is also concerned with establishing and managing procedures that control who has access, how it is kept up to date and how it is kept secure.

2 It helps protect the security of the information held, and also the integrity of the data.

3 Any three of: formulating ICT company policies; installing hardware and software; deciding and recommending the hardware and software that should be purchased; training; user guides; maintenance of the system; keeping up to date with advances in ICT.

4 Any three of: the network installed affects the speed at which data can be transmitted; the drives used affect the amount of data that can be stored, and the speed at which it can be accessed; processor speed and memory capacity affect the speed at which the system works; appropriate input devices ensure the most efficient data entry methods can be used.

5 Any three of: folder structures; folder names; file names; version control procedures; back-up procedures; delete and archive (housekeeping) procedures.

6 Any three of: time wasted finding files; wrong or old version of a file being used, resulting in a wrong decision being made; data being lost because of poor back-up procedure; disks becoming full if old files are not deleted or archived.

Quick Questions 5

1 Security – protecting against theft, damage and destruction. Integrity – ensuring data is accurate, up to date and error free.

2 Ensuring that only staff who need to know what the data is do know. This can mean restricting access to the data to only those staff that need access, and also ensuring that staff who do have access to the data do not discuss it with others.

3 Theft – lock offices; close windows; padlock systems on desks; install CCTV/security cameras. Accidental damage – don't let staff move equipment; provide trolleys when equipment does need to be moved; discourage staff from eating and drinking at their computer. Damage from fire or flood – ensure staff are aware of any fire/flood hazards and take steps to prevent them, e.g. no smoking in premises; fire doors to stop spread of fire.

4 If server or other computer is stolen, data may be lost. If back-ups are not taken regularly, e.g. daily, back-up disks may contain out-of-date information.

5 Any two of: put papers back in filing cabinet; collect papers from printer; shred papers that are to be destroyed; tidy papers off your desk at night.

Quick Questions 6

1 Any three of: Data must be – fairly and lawfully obtained and processed; accurate and up to date; adequate, relevant and not excessive; processed for limited purposes; held securely; not retained for longer than necessary; processed in accordance with the individual's rights; not be transferred to countries outside the EU unless the country has adequate protection for the individual.

2 Any one of: subject access (you can find out what is held on computer about you); prevent processing (you can ask a data controller not to process your information); direct marketing (you can ask that your data is not used for direct marketing); automatic decision making (you can object to decisions being made on your behalf on account of the data held); compensation (you can claim compensation for damage or distress if the Act is breached); rectify, block, erase and destroy (you can apply to court to order a data controller to do these if the data is not accurate or has opinions based on inaccurate information).

3 Beside the photocopier.

4 Examples include: not having enough licences to cover the number of users; using illegal software, e.g. copies obtained from a disreputable source.

5 Any one of: unauthorised access to computer material; unauthorised access with the intention of committing further offences; unauthorised modification of computer material.

ANSWERS TO EXTENDED RESPONSE QUESTIONS

1 Effectiveness in the workplace

1 To gain the 10 marks in this question you must discuss different methods used by the administrator, giving potential advantages or disadvantages of the methods suggested. These should focus on *supervising*, that is, the decision-making and delegating aspects, and then on the *organising*, which is the developing, motivation and control of activities. Make sure that you expand your answer by suggesting actions that can be taken, and give examples.

2 It is not enough to list what a PDP is or does to get marks. You are asked to justify – so you need to say why an action is a good thing, don't just say what the action is. For example, you could say that a PDP could be used to highlight areas for development. To justify this action you would need to go on and say why this might be a good thing – you could go on to say that it helps identify areas where training and support are necessary, and by offering the employee appropriate training and development opportunities, their personal performance should improve (which has obvious benefits to the organisation).

3 When you describe something, give your example and then a description of it (don't just list examples). In this answer you would be expected to mention that maybe targets had not been clearly understood, and then explain why – perhaps the task was beyond the experience or capability of the employee. In a 6-mark question you would probably get one mark for each example and one mark for the description of each.

4 Discuss – give advantages and/or disadvantages and expand your answer to show that you understand the potential consequences. For example, if targets are not set then employees may spend too much time completing tasks. This can result in time and resources being wasted and deadlines being missed, both of which may affect other activities within the organisation.

5 Identify and describe – any three time stealers could be selected as long as an explanation of each with an example is given.

6 Describe – identify the benefits and concerns that employees may have and then explain why each is a benefit or concern. For example, a benefit of belonging to a team is that you can share knowledge and skills. This means that you can help each other out if things are really busy. A concern might be personality clashes, which may result in staff being unpleasant to each other or obstructive, resulting in poor performance from the team.

2 Work practices and the modern working environment

1 Discuss – give advantages and disadvantages if possible. Develop the points that will be different in the new environment, e.g. staff will not be able to personalise their work space. This may have the effect of employees feeling uncomfortable in their working environment or lacking respect for the workspace, as they don't feel ownership. For 6 marks you should discuss 3 potential differences and their effects.

2 Discuss – give advantages and disadvantages if possible. You should identify a work practice, e.g. homeworking, and then explain how it offers the employee and the employer a greater degree of flexibility. For 8 marks, try to give 4 examples.

3 Identify and describe – give an example and an explanation. You could name some of the effects felt by staff, e.g. headaches and sore throats. The main emphasis of your answer is the checks that companies should take, e.g. make sure heating and ventilation controls are available and effective, and then go on to explain why this can help, e.g. a well-ventilated environment that is not too hot or cold will help staff feel more comfortable. For 8 marks, try to give 4 examples.

4 Describe – give an example and an explanation of each point. The question asks for costs and benefits, so make sure you identify at least one cost and one benefit. For example, a benefit of homeworking might be that as it offers staff with personal commitments (e.g. children or older relatives) the chance to work more flexibly, it allows the employer to retain valuable well-trained staff. A cost to the employer might be that staff are not always in the office so it may be difficult to cope when other staff are on holiday or off sick. For 6 marks you should describe at least 3 costs/benefits.

5 Justify – give reasons. For example, it is cheap in terms of time and commitment from the employers' point of view. For 4 marks, give 4 reasons.

6 Discuss – identify the consequences and then explain the effect it might have on the employee. For example, the employee may be dismissed, and this would have serious financial consequences.

3 Recruiting, developing and supporting staff

1 Justify – give reasons why a course of action would be taken, e.g. recruiting for a new post internally would be less expensive than advertising externally.

2 Discuss – give examples and explain advantages and disadvantages or strengths and weaknesses. For example, if the interviewer doesn't prepare properly, they might ask the wrong questions, with the result that they may choose a candidate who is not really suitable for the post. If the interviewee isn't well prepared they may be late for the interview which may result in them missing the interview altogether.

3 Describe – identify and explain a benefit, e.g. the appraisal system helps the employer to set targets which in turn enables them to measure employee performance.

4 Compare – identify the different forms of external training and say how they are different/similar. For example, attending lectures/tutorials at college day release means that the member of staff needs time off work whereas online learning using a PC and software training programme means that the member of staff can study at work or home (so may not be absent from work so much).

5 Discuss – use examples and give advantages and disadvantages. For example, an absence management system could enable the employer to keep in regular contact with an absent employee, encouraging the employee to return to work as soon as they felt well enough.

6 Describe – give an example and a description, e.g. work–life balance is about the individual being in control over where, when and how they work and balancing work with other commitments in their life. It may include flexible working patterns, e.g. working from home, part-time hours, and school holiday leave. It is about the employee having the opportunity to enjoy a healthy but balanced working life along with time for themselves and their families.

4 Meetings

1 Explain – an ad hoc is a committee set up for a specific purpose. Describe – identify and explain the other types of committee meeting, e.g. Advisory committee gives advice on specific issues, such as moving to new premises.

2   Compare – discuss the similarities or differences between the two. For example, for an external meeting factors such as location, parking, and cost/budget would need to be considered, whereas an internal meeting venue would be cheaper, would require less travel but may not offer adequate facilities. For both, refreshments and dietary issues need to be considered.

3   Justify – give reasons for doing something. For example, it is important to produce minutes of a formal meeting because they provide an accurate record of the proceedings which can be referred to later for details of follow-up actions.

4   Outline – identify the possible consequences of inadequate preparation and give a brief description. For example, there may be a technical fault, e.g. the connection fails, with the result that the meeting can't take place. Failing to take account of time differences with international conferences may make it difficult for some people to attend.

5   Identify the qualities, e.g. tact, diplomacy, respected, fair but firm. Describe or explain the significance of these qualities, e.g. needs to be able to control the meeting, giving everyone a fair share.

6   Discuss – list the uses, e.g. email, e-diaries, video conferencing, then explain why they are advantages and how they facilitate meetings, e.g. video conferencing means people can attend meetings without having to travel as much, reducing travel costs and environmental damage.

5   Effective customer service

1   Compare – note the differences and similarities between benefits to the organisation and the customer. Identify benefits and give a brief description, e.g. benefits to organisation include customer loyalty, improved reputation, increased market share, whereas the benefits to the customer could include reliable quality, feeling of being valued, good choice, well trained staff.

2   Identify and describe – give examples of the key points and then explain what they mean. For example, all complaints should be treated seriously and logged, which ensures that the complaint isn't lost in the system, and staff know when it was made so that they can try to resolve the situation within a reasonable time scale.

3   Compare – note the differences and similarities. Explain what a mystery shopper is and say how this differs from a customer focus group. For example, a mystery shopper will experience the same service and treatment as a regular customer and will then feed back their experience, whereas a customer focus group is a group of people brought together to answer specific questions and give responses. This method is more expensive and takes more time.

4   Justify – explain what IIP is and give reasons why it is a good idea. For example, training needs of businesses awarded IIP status are more closely linked to business objectives, resulting in better trained staff, so performance and productivity are improved.

5   Suggest – put forward a recommendation or advise on a course of action. For example, the company could conduct a customer satisfaction survey to help them identify their strengths and weaknesses, which they could then act on.

6   Discuss – explain what it is and give advantages and disadvantages if possible. For example, when dealing face to face with a customer, they can see you as well as hear you, so your body language is just as important as your tone of voice. On the telephone, it is important that you use the right tone of voice as this is all your customer has to judge you on.

6 The role of information in decision making

1 Explain what each term means (1 mark per explanation) and relate it to quality information (1 mark per example per term). For example, concise means that something is to the point and doesn't include unnecessary detail. This is important so that the person reading the information can concentrate on the important issue and not be distracted by unnecessary detail.

2 Identify each level of management, e.g. strategic, tactical and operational, then give an appropriate example of the type of decision taken at each level, e.g. deciding whether or not to take over another company is a strategic decision.

3 Compare – explain similarities and differences. Define qualitative and quantitative information, then develop the answer to show how the two differ, giving illustrative examples.

4 Justify – select any two stages in the data processing cycle, then state why each stage is relevant, give reasons for it, and state the consequences or implications to the organisation if it is not taken. For example, the stage of checking is important because it is necessary to confirm that the collected information is correct. If information is not checked carefully the organisation may be working with incomplete, incorrect or out-of-date data, which can result in wrong decisions being made, because they are based on poor quality information.

5 Discuss – identify at least one strength and one weakness, then develop the answer to show or explain why each point is a strength or weakness.

7 The impact of ICT on work practices and management of information

1 Discuss – give examples and advantages and disadvantages if possible. For example, one advantage of ICT is that information can be accessed and distributed more efficiently, easily and quickly. In terms of the impact in each area – input, processing and output – if systems are well set up, data need be input only once (e.g. in a database), it can be processed in different ways for different purposes (e.g. searches, reports), and different outputs produced (letters, reports, etc.). This means that tasks can be done more quickly, making the organisation more efficient and productive.

2 Describe – give an example and an explanation. For example, data can be presented logically, perhaps grouped and/or sorted in different ways, making it relatively easy to find the information required and to understand the data presented.

3 Justify – give reasons for taking a course of action. For example, an e-business solution enables the company to reach a global market without having to open premises or employ staff in different countries. So the organisation could expand without greatly increasing its costs.

4 Identify and suggest – give an example and advise on a course of action. For example, theft is a security risk; a preventative step could be an intruder alarm.

5 Discuss – give examples and advantages and disadvantages. For example, poor electronic file management could result in a haphazard folder structure being used to store company documents. This could result in staff having difficulty in locating the files that they need.

6 Identify and suggest – give an example and advise on a course of action. For example, under the Data Protection Act 1984 and 1998, staff should do everything they can to protect the security of the data, e.g. logging off when they leave their computer (so that unauthorised users can't access their files).

INDEX